Creative Play Therapy with Adolescents and Adults

This practical, user-friendly manual shows mental health professionals how to implement play therapy with adolescents and adults and how to conceptualize client struggles using a wealth of creative approaches.

Creative Play Therapy with Adolescents and Adults follows an accessible seven-stage process for professionals to address clients' core needs and establish an empathic therapeutic relationship. The book charts the stages of play therapy and explores a range of expressive arts including art, drama, dance, writing and sand play and the key materials needed for each. It also considers additional aspects of play therapy including resistance, spirituality and self-care. Filled with techniques, skills and case studies to help demystify complex client work, the book outlines an easy-to-follow treatment protocol for healing and resolution.

This book will be of interest to a wide range of mental health professionals working with adults and adolescents as it encourages a more creative career and lasting, tangible progress in clients.

Denis' A. Thomas, PhD, NCC, is an associate professor at Lipscomb University. She is the lead faculty for the play therapy specialization and faculty director of the Lipscomb University Center for Play Therapy and Expressive Arts. She is a host of the podcast *Play Therapy Across the Lifespan*, the author of 20 journal and magazine articles and a regular presenter at national and international conferences.

Melanie H. Morris, PhD, is an associate professor at Lipscomb University and a licenced psychologist and health service provider in Tennessee. Melanie serves as the clinical director for the Master of Science in Clinical Mental Health Counseling.

Creative Play Therapy with Adolescents and Adults

Moving from Helping to Healing

DENIS' A. THOMAS AND MELANIE H. MORRIS

Routledge
Taylor & Francis Group

NEW YORK AND LONDON

First published 2020
by Routledge
52 Vanderbilt Avenue, New York, NY 10017

and by Routledge
2 Park Square, Milton Park, Abingdon, Oxon, OX14 4RN

Routledge is an imprint of the Taylor & Francis Group, an informa business

Library of Congress Cataloging-in-Publication Data
Names: Thomas, Denis' A., author. | Morris, Melanie H., author.
Title: Creative play therapy with adolescents and adults : moving from
    helping to healing / Denis' A. Thomas and Melanie H. Morris.
Description: New York, NY : Routledge, 2020. | Includes bibliographical
    references and index.
Identifiers: LCCN 2019058161 (print) | LCCN 2019058162 (ebook) | ISBN
    9781138615281 (hardback) | ISBN 9781138615298 (paperback) | ISBN
    9780429449307 (ebook)
Subjects: LCSH: Play therapy.
Classification: LCC RJ505.P6 T45 2020 (print) | LCC RJ505.P6 (ebook) |
    DDC 616.89/1653—dc23
LC record available at https://lccn.loc.gov/2019058161
LC ebook record available at https://lccn.loc.gov/2019058162

ISBN: 978-1-138-61528-1 (hbk)
ISBN: 978-1-138-61529-8 (pbk)
ISBN: 978-0-429-44930-7 (ebk)

Typeset in Dante and Avenir
by Swales & Willis, Exeter, Devon, UK

Contents

Figures

Tables

A Letter from the Authors

Writing this book has been an exciting experience solidifying concepts we have been teaching for years. As we slowed down to thoughtfully consider exactly how we do the work we do, how we teach others to do this work and how to integrate essential skills with the body of professional literature and research, the book you are holding is the result. Grounded in both theory and experience, Creative Play Therapy is rooted in Child-Centered Play Therapy, but extends that treatment approach to adolescents and adults.

In writing a practical how-to book for practitioners, one of the challenges is containing the great diversity of personalities, professions and experiences into a "normal" linear therapy process, which only perfectly exists in theory. The processes are based on hundreds of professional experiences, but those are not without variance. Sometimes, work with a client looks similar to the stages outlined in this book, and sometimes, a client may weave back and forth through stages multiple times. The client-centered approach is rooted in a trust that the client knows how to do the work that needs to be done. The client knows how to proceed in the best way for that particular client, and this book will never supersede that. Knowing the stages helps you facilitate the therapeutic work and become comfortable with what happens in each stage, but the stages are not a fixed seven-step path. Likewise, the term *therapist* will be used to refer to the one in the professional helping role, whether that be a mental health counselor, psychologist, marriage and family therapist, social worker or other trained professional. Language is limiting, but we have done our best to use language that is helpful rather than hindering.

This challenge of presenting one therapeutic approach is compounded by the therapist's unique skills and experience in the profession. We all have our favorite techniques and therapeutic phrases that we tend to use. Ours are included in suggestions throughout this book, but you may adapt them or pick and choose only the ones that work for you. This book does not seek to provide a rigid protocol on how Creative Play Therapy must be administered (absolutely not!), just a suggested, easy to implement approach to therapeutic work where your unique abilities can flourish. This is, after all, a creative approach, not a cookie-cutter template.

Therefore, use the content in this book as a guide. Adapt what you learn to your style of helping and what works with your clients. Bring the expressive arts that you most enjoy into your work, even if you use one that is not presented in this book. If we believe clients have what they need to do the work they need to do, we also believe that you have what you need to facilitate that work. Trust yourself as you learn to sharpen your skills and deepen your knowledge. You will not do this perfectly – no one does, not even the authors of this book. We believe that your imperfections make you more relatable to clients (but with a gentle warning not to let imperfections turn into impairments which can be harmful to clients). You need to know the difference. Therapeutic work is dependent on the counselor as the tool, so Chapter 15 will provide a helpful framework for self-care.

Healing (Stage 6 of the process) is not dependent on your impeccable use of this treatment modality, and, in fact, perfectionism will be counter-productive to the healing work you seek to facilitate with your clients. You cannot authentically believe that it is okay for the client to be wounded and imperfect while demanding perfection from yourself. Healing is dependent on your working relationship with the client, and that includes much that is contained in this book, but also a few things that are not, so it will not be a perfect process. Let that be a relief to you, if you struggle with trying to do this the "right" way. Therapists with the most successful outcomes are not those who present a pristine, professional exterior to clients, but those who embody authenticity, those who have also experienced pain and those who can be guides for the journey because they know the path.

It is our sincere hope that as you learn and apply the concepts of Creative Play Therapy, it boosts confidence in your ability to help others. You are enough. You bring your unique blend of education, skills, talents and life experience to this creative work to help your clients in ways that are as unique as you are. We also hope that you see transformational work in your clients, and as they heal, you change not only an individual, but those around that individual, too. This makes your work very meaningful. Finally, it is our desire that as you learn to facilitate Creative Play Therapy, you also learn to value creatively caring for yourself, too. This profession needs highly skilled professionals changing lives with a career's worth of experience. May you grow into that kind of helper.

Denis' A. Thomas
Melanie H. Morris

Acknowledgments

When you get to fulfill a dream of writing a book on a topic that you are passionate about, and you have the gift of a sabbatical to write it while traveling in a motorhome with your family, there are lots of people to thank.

First, I want to thank my co-author, Melanie, whose contributions made this final manuscript much better than what I could do on my own. Thank you for agreeing to write this with me, for being an amazing colleague and a better friend. You have contributed to our play therapy program from the beginning, and it's better, too, because of you.

Second, I want to thank Lipscomb University (really, the people there) who believed in me and supported me as I began teaching these ideas. I have a lifetime of gratitude for the sabbatical space to write and rest. This also includes the colleagues in my program who picked up the slack – Drs. Jake and Melanie Morris, Douglas Ribeiro and DeAndrea Witherspoon-Nash. Thank you to the rest of the department, too, including department chair Dr. Shanna Ray. I love working with people that I truly like and respect. Thanks to Dr. Holly Allen for inspiring my daily writing habit, and Dr. Leonard Allen for sharing his publishing expertise. I could go on, but I will end with a special thank you to Kathi Johnson and Jenna Vance who go above and beyond. I fly farther because of you all.

I want to express my gratefulness to our graduate assistants, especially Madison Natarajan, Cara Allison and Rachel Sellers. Madison, thanks for creating order and helping start this project. Cara, thanks for your fabulous attention to detail, especially near deadlines. Rachel, thanks for your contribution to the neuroscience section and your enthusiasm for research.

Thank you to Dr. Jeff Cochran, who taught my first play therapy class, and the Nashville play therapy community who continues to teach me now.

Thanks to my editors and the staff at Routledge Publishing. This book is something that I have wanted to do for a long time, and it's exciting and humbling to be asked to write it.

Most importantly, thank you to my husband, Tim, and children, A, Z and ZA, for giving me time to write even as my heart tugs me to you. You will always be the biggest gifts in my life. Our traveling time together as I wrote was the best.

Denis' A. Thomas

Thank you, Denis', for inviting me to join you on this endeavor. I value my relationship with you as a colleague and a dear friend. What a blessing to have both in my daily professional life. Your commitment to creative play therapy is admirable. You are very capably training the next generation of play therapists in our community and inspiring them to love their careers where they can use their own creative talents to help their clients heal. Our students are lucky to have you. I appreciate your faith in my abilities and your continual encouragement for me to push myself and try new things.

Thank you, Dr. Jake Morris, our program director and my husband, for your confidence in my abilities and for your encouragement to pursue any dream I have. It is a blessing to have a spouse who believes in you more than you believe in yourself. I am thankful that he and Dr. Shanna Ray, our department chair, allow us as faculty the intellectual freedom to determine our own projects and pursuits. We have felt their support all the way.

I am grateful to my parents who live near us and support me in all of my endeavors. Their continual support has allowed me to reach all of my dreams in life.

Thank you to my children who are patient with me as I pursue excellence in my work. I pray that I can be your best possible mother. I love you both dearly.

Melanie H. Morris

Introduction
An Overview of the Field of Play Therapy

Before moving into the new treatment modality of Creative Play Therapy, we want to first begin with a brief overview of the field of play therapy. Most of this will not be new knowledge for those practicing in the field, but for those who are students or beginners, it may help to understand the history of the profession and the effectiveness of it. We also want to explain why it works, offer a few insights from the field of neuroscience, and explain child-centered play therapy. We will draw from this information later in the book. Finally, we will end the introduction with an overview of what to expect in the coming pages of the book.

History of Play Therapy

Play therapy began as a way to provide age and developmentally appropriate therapeutic services to children. In the early years of psychotherapy, lying on a couch and free associating with psychoanalyst was helpful for adults, but professionals quickly realized that children needed something different. Since children naturally played, and views on childhood were changing, play became a bridge to providing psychotherapy to children, including children under the age of six.

In 1911, H. G. Wells, author of *The Time Machine* and *War of the Worlds*, published a book of floor games (Wells, 2017). He listed four categories of toys, the kinds of toys played with repeatedly and in many different ways. He suggested that the categories of toys were 1) soldiers (including sailors, railway porters, civilians and lower animals); 2) bricks; 3) boards and planks; and 4) railway trains and rails (along with miscellaneous things like tin ships and Easter eggs). Wells believed these types of games not only kept boys and girls happy (entertainment), but also built a "framework of spacious and inspiring ideas" (p. 53). His book reflected a broader shift that valued play, and play soon became integrated with therapy.

Melanie Klein, a contemporary of the first credited child psychoanalyst Hermine Hug-Hellmuth, first began applying what she later called the psychoanalytic play technique in 1919 with a 5-year-old boy (Klein, 1955). She wrote, "In interpreting not only the child's words but also his activities with his toys, I applied this basic principle [free association] to the mind of the child, whose play and varied activities, in fact his whole behavior, are means of expressing what the adult expresses predominantly by words" (pp. 223–224).

In the context of history, Wells and Klein voiced an idea about childhood that had finally taken hold in Europe. For about 150 years, the climate had slowly been shifting from seeing children as little adults to appreciating children as fundamentally different from adults. This led to a rise in professional interest in play (Ray, 2011). Conceptualizing children differently opened the door to interventions occurring in childhood to improve their future. This could be done through enriching activities (such as floor games), through prevention, or through therapy for childhood problems to reduce the impact in adulthood.

Over the last hundred years, the methodologies of using play to provide therapy with children have greatly expanded. Now, popular approaches identify with different theories (child-centered, Adlerian, object relations, Jungian, gestalt, reality, and others), different client groups (individual, family, siblings, group), and different settings (therapy offices, schools, homes, hospitals, the outdoors, and more). The body of play therapy research is growing and broadening. We have learned much from tapping into play to help children. Now, it is time to expand that work across the lifespan, drawing on the benefits for children, and applying it to adolescents and adults.

Effectiveness of Play Therapy

Treatment is defined by the American Psychological Association (APA, 2012) as, "any process in which a trained healthcare provider offers assistance based upon his or her professional expertise to a person who has a problem that is defined as related to 'health' or 'wellness'" (p. 1). While many different treatments are effective, effectiveness varies from client to client, disorder to disorder, and helper to helper (Kenney-Noziska et al., 2012), so like all treatments, play therapy is not a magical modality that works with every client every time, but it is a developmentally responsive and empirically supported treatment (Wheeler & Dillman Taylor, 2016).

Dr. Sue Bratton has compiled summaries of empirical research studies in play therapy at the Evidence Based Child Therapy web site (http://evidence-basedchildtherapy.com). We refer you there for a comprehensive list of play therapy peer-reviewed research. One noteworthy portion is a summary of meta-analytic research (Lin & Bratton, n.d.). A meta-analysis looks at data from a number of independent studies on a subject to determine trends and usually to examine the consistency of treatment. By compiling data from many smaller studies, researchers pool together a larger sample.

Four of these meta-analyses (Bratton et al., 2005; Leblanc & Ritchie, 2001; Lin & Bratton, 2015; Ray et al., 2015) demonstrated robust evidence for the treatment effect of play therapy, with statistically significant effect sizes for behavioral problems, social adjustment, personality concerns, self-concept, anxiety and fear, developmental concerns, and parent/child relationships. They found that play therapy was effective in schools, outpatient clinics, residential settings, and critical-incident settings. It worked with individuals and groups. Many of the research studies included used child-centered play therapy, and those results suggested that CCPT is also a culturally responsive intervention.

In other words, play therapy works. It works for a variety of presenting concerns. It works across various settings. It works with individuals and groups. And it adapts well with clients (and therapists) from different cultural backgrounds. Although debate has raged for decades about whether directive or nondirective approaches are more effective, they are equally effective at producing therapeutic change (Kenney-Noziska et al., 2012).

Why Play Therapy Works

Now that you know the research has established that play therapy works, the next question is how it works. What is it about playing within a therapeutic context that provides such clear benefits to clients? First, to answer the questions of how and why play therapy works, Drewes and Schaefer (2016) listed 20 therapeutic powers of play. They wrote:

> These play powers appear to constitute or augment the healing process, rather than simply serving as a medium for the application of other

treatment modalities that just use play as an adjunct to the protocol. In other words, play powers are the actual change agents, not just an aid in moderating treatment.

(p. 38)

According to the authors, play accomplishes four important healing actions: facilitating communication, fostering emotional wellness, enhancing social relationships, and increasing personal strengths. This happens through at least 20 mechanisms described in the *Handbook of Play Therapy* (Drewes & Schaefer, 2016).

- Play facilitates *communication* through self-expression, access to the unconscious, direct teaching, and indirect teaching.
- Play fosters *emotional wellness* through catharsis, abreaction (repressed memories brought into the consciousness and released), positive emotions, counterconditioning of fears, stress inoculation, and stress management.
- Play enhances *social relationships* through therapeutic relationship, attachment, sense of self and empathy.
- Play increases *personal strengths* through creative problem solving, resiliency, moral development, accelerated psychological development, self-regulation, and self-esteem.

While these play powers are healing, they do not occur in a vacuum. They occur within the context of a therapeutic relationship between the client and the therapist. The play powers explain why play is therapeutic, but it does not explain why some therapists are more effective at facilitating positive outcomes. Therefore, the second factor in understanding why play therapy works is the relationship between the therapist and the client. This emotional bond is the core to lasting and productive change (Green et al., 2013). Those therapists who are most adept at creating psychologically safe places and conveying unconditional acceptance allow clients to explore and initiate deeper change. The quality of the relationship is more important to clients than interventions or techniques, and the client's experience of feeling empathically understood is considered the best predictor of a successful outcome (Mancillas, 2006).

The third consideration in understanding why play therapy works is the externalization of the issue, but within the perspective of the present time. When playing, the client is able to experience, as Etzi (2004) described, the paradox of the play being real and not real at the same time. This means that the client can "entertain a provisional reality with the optimal distance from reality constraints" (p. 243).

Clients can, in a sense, take out the issue or core need, look at it from a third person perspective, use the resources available to them in the present that may have been absent in the past, and test out what change might look like. The distance creates the safety to risk doing this. Etzi (2004) wrote: "Playful enactments of inner emotional conflicts in therapy allow oneself and the other to be acknowledged and accepted as separate and valuable persons in an experiential and immediate sense" (p. 247).

The answer, then, to how play therapy works is three-fold. It includes the inherent power in play, within the context of a safe therapeutic relationship, and from a perspective where the client is able to explore through a provisional reality. Creative Play Therapy also uses the powers of play, the safety of the therapeutic relationship, and the space to explore past, present and future realities with adolescents and adults.

Play Therapy and Neuroscience

The growing body of literature on neuroscience is beyond the scope of this book and these authors, but a basic knowledge may improve your therapeutic presence, help you advocate for clients, and explain the power of play to others (Wheeler & Dillman Taylor, 2016). As you probably know, the brain contains two hemispheres, the right and left sides of the brain. The right brain houses emotional intelligence, creativity, imagination, and intuition. The left brain computes numbers, logic, analytical thinking, and language. The corpus callosum joins the two hemispheres with a band of nerve fibers. Recent developments in the field of neuroscience (Porges, 2011; Siegel, 2010) support play therapy as an effective treatment modality that rewires the brain and promotes both physical and emotional healing.

We now have a better understanding of the nervous system and neuroplasticity, the development of new connections within the brain from new experiences and stimuli. We also know more about the profound biological impact of safe and emotionally attuned relationships from the field of neuroscience (Porges, 2015). These research advances support the benefits and legitimacy of play therapy with all ages, and it provides deeper insight into how this creative treatment modality transforms people's lives.

Our nervous system, our body, is neurobiologically wired to sense safety or danger in our environment. If danger is detected, the body moves into a sympathetic fight or flight state, becoming hyperaroused. The body may feel anxious, irritable, impulsive, or reactive. If the feeling of danger is not resolved, the body may move into a state of hypoarousal, activating the parasympathetic freeze response. The body may disconnect, dissociate, numb, or shut down (Porges, 2011).

However, neuroscientists have discovered what is referred to as the Social Engagement System, a system that is activated when the body is calm and safe (Porges, 2011; Siegel, 2010). When the nervous system is soothed, we are able to play, rest, and connect with others. In this space, we have greater physiological flexibility and consequently, opportunities for change. When this system is engaged, clients are able to remain in what Siegel (2010) called the "window of tolerance." In this space, we can help clients self-soothe, emotionally regulate, and remain present and mindful in the optimal state of arousal in the therapy session. Play is an excellent modality to lead clients to the window of tolerance and help them remain there.

Activating the social engagement system and creating a window of tolerance is the prerequisite to create new neural pathways because it establishes the optimal chemical environment for change. Play is an engaging experience that impacts hormone secretion, which changes our physiology and our brains. Play increases levels of oxytocin, a hormone that enhances feelings of wellbeing and trust, which helps foster a relationship between the therapist and the client, one of the powers of play (Drewes & Schaefer, 2016). When the therapist offers emotional attunement through supportive comments and an over-all presence of warmth and compassion, oxytocin and dopamine are released and enable neuroplasticity, shaping brain circuits and healing the body (Cozolino, 2017).

A safe relationship is a powerful, if not the most powerful, neurobiological intervention (Perry, 2006), once again emphasizing that the relationship is *the* therapy. Play therapy fosters a secure attachment pattern between the therapist and the client. When a client feels safe, the therapist can assist the client in emotional regulation through a process called mirroring. Mirror neurons enable us to self-regulate through co-regulation and mirroring, or imitating another person (Iacoboni, 2003). As the therapist offers a calming presence, mirror neurons grant the client the capacity for self-regulation and acceptance of emotion. Clients can then use the safety of the relationship to approach difficult emotional states and revisit pain and unresolved trauma, while developing adaptive coping responses (Perry, 2006; Siegel, 2010).

Current research has revealed that trauma and even seemingly benign life stressors cause dysregulation not only to the brain, but to the entire nervous system (van der Kolk, 2014). Play therapy aims to regulate the body and the mind, to bring back a sense of homeostasis to a person's entire being. Using a safe, therapeutic relationship as an anchor, the play therapist is able to help the client achieve optimal levels of arousal, that window of tolerance, laying the groundwork for lasting and positive physiological change.

All of this points to a need for interventions for adolescents and adults that support them physiologically as well as emotionally, and interventions that heal physically and emotionally, but they must exist within the context of a psychologically safe therapeutic relationship. In Creative Play Therapy, we propose that play therapy drawing heavily from the expressive arts provides on option to do this. More on that in Chapter 1.

What Is Child-Centered Play Therapy?

One treatment, child-centered play therapy, integrated the young field of play therapy with the theoretical orientation of Carl Rogers' person-centered theory. Rogers originally called his theoretical approach nondirective therapy, then changed the name to client-centered therapy to reflect his clinical work, and as he applied the philosophy to all relationships, he settled on the name person-centered therapy (Rogers, 1980). The child-centered approach is not merely a series of techniques or protocol, but a way of being (Mullen & Rickli, 2014). Virginia Axline operationalized Rogers' philosophy and principles and applied them to relationships with children (Landreth, 2012) establishing child-centered play therapy. She believed that children also experienced the freedom for growth through the secure relationship between the therapist and the client.

Landreth (2012) claimed that:

> Although there are several well-established theoretical approaches to play therapy, among those in current use, child-centered play therapy has the longest history of use, the strongest research support, and according to recent surveys of practicing play therapists, is most used by play therapy practitioners.
>
> (pp. 34–35)

Child-centered play therapy is a nondirective approach and requires the therapist's deep commitment to the belief that children are able to grow towards health, or self-actualization (Glover & Landreth, 2016). It is a complete therapeutic system based on the deep and abiding belief that children are resilient and capable of being self-directive (Landreth, 2012).

Creative Play Therapy is grounded in the person-centered theoretical approach and is heavily influenced by child-centered play therapy. However, we extend that knowledge and research to older adolescents and adults. We believe that play serves the six purposes outlined by Ray (2011) of fun, symbolic expression, catharsis, social development, mastery, and a release of energy for adults. With adults, play still has the capacity to facilitate communication, foster emotional wellness, enhance social relationships, and increase personal strengths through the 20 powers of play mechanisms (Drewes & Schaefer, 2016). When it occurs within the context of a safe, therapeutic relationship and provides the space to risk exploring what is not real in the present reality, it is highly effective with adults, too.

What to Expect from This Book

In Part 1, Creative Play Therapy and Core Issues, we provide the foundation for understanding Creative Play Therapy. Chapter 1 defines play therapy and extends it to working with adolescents and adults, introduces expressive arts, and provides an overview of Creative Play Therapy. Chapter 2 describes expressive arts, materials needed, and how to externalize internal perceptions. Chapter 3 explains how Creative Play Therapy extends the benefits of traditional talk therapy. Chapter 4 introduces core needs, themes often seen around them, and how to identify them. Chapter 5 places Creative Play Therapy against the backdrop of physical, psychosocial, cognitive, moral and spiritual development across the lifespan.

In Part 2, Stages of Creative Play Therapy, we spend a chapter on each of the seven stages. These are peppered with skills, case studies and sample dialogs. Each chapter also includes a creative technique, a procedure initiated by the helper to achieve therapeutic goals (Peabody & Schaefer, 2016), for practical application.

In Part 3, Additional Aspects of Play Therapy, we spend a chapter each reevaluating resistance, exploring spirituality, and addressing wellness.

Throughout the book, you will find examples to help with applying the concepts. Some are sample dialogues, some are first person case studies written by people who have experienced Creative Play Therapy, and some are practical ideas to try. We have intentionally stayed away from explicit material which can add to compassion fatigue. Instead, we use the term complex trauma, which means severe and prolonged exposure to childhood interpersonal trauma (Olson-Morrison, 2017). When working with complex trauma, we find Creative Play Therapy to be powerful in facilitating healing, but for the sake of learning, we use less complex, and potentially triggering, examples.

This chapter provided a short summary of the field of play therapy: the history, why play therapy is effective, and how neuroscience supports it. We also wanted to explain child-centered play therapy, since Creative Play is built on those foundational tenets. Many other books have been written on these subjects, so our aim here was to provide just enough information to serve as foundational for the rest of the book. In condensing this information, we have necessarily omitted aspects, but our goal is only to provide a brief background. We encourage you to read the authors cited for more in depth information. Now, let's turn to Creative Play Therapy, a treatment modality for adolescents and adults.

References

APA. (2012). *Recognition of psychotherapy effectiveness*. Retrieved from https://search.ebscohost.com/login.aspx?direct=true&AuthType=sso&db=psyh&AN=2013-30990-003&site=ehost-live&custid=s8863735

Bratton, S. C., Ray, D., Rhine, T., & Jones, L. (2005). The efficacy of play therapy with children: A meta-analytic review of treatment outcomes. *Professional Psychology: Research and Practice, 36*(4), 376–390. doi:10.1037/0735-7028.36.4.376

Cozolino, L. (2017). *The neuroscience of psychotherapy: Healing the social brain* (3rd ed.). New York, NY: W W Norton & Co.

Drewes, A. A., & Schaefer, C. E. (2016). The therapeutic powers of play. In K. J. O'Connor, C. E. Schaefer, & L. D. Braverman (Eds.), *Handbook of play therapy* (2nd ed., pp. 35–60). Hoboken, NJ: John Wiley & Sons Inc.

Etzi, J. (2004). Analysis of play. *The Humanistic Psychologist, 32*(Summer), 239–256.

Glover, G., & Landreth, G. L. (2016). Child-centered play therapy. In K. J. O'Connor, C. E. Schaefer, & L. D. Braverman (Eds.), *Handbook of play therapy* (2nd ed., pp. 93–118). Hoboken, NJ: John Wiley & Sons Inc.

Green, E. J., Myrick, A. C., & Crenshaw, D. A. (2013). Toward secure attachment in adolescent relational development: Advancements from sandplay and expressive play-based interventions. *International Journal of Play Therapy, 22*(2), 90–102. doi:10.1037/a0032323

Iacoboni, M. (2003). Understanding intentions through imitation. In S. H. Johnson-Frey (Ed.), *Taking action: Cognitive neuroscience perspectives on intentional acts*, (pp. 107–138). Cambridge, MA: The MIT Press.

Kenney-Noziska, S. G., Schaefer, C. E., & Homeyer, L. E. (2012). Beyond directive or nondirective: Moving the conversation forward. *International Journal of Play Therapy, 21*(4), 244–252. doi:10.1037/a0028910

Klein, M. (1955). The psychoanalytic play technique. *American Journal of Orthopsychiatry, 25*(2), 223–237. doi:10.1111/j.1939-0025.1955.tb00131.x

Landreth, G. L. (2012). *Play therapy: The art of the relationship* (3rd. ed.). New York: Routledge.

Leblanc, M., & Ritchie, M. (2001). A meta-analysis of play therapy outcomes. *Counselling Psychology Quarterly, 14*(2), 149–163. doi:10.1080/09515070110059142

Lin, Y. W., & Bratton, S. C. (2015). A meta-analytic review of child-centered play therapy approaches. *Journal of Counseling & Development, 93*(1), 45–58. doi:10.1002/j.1556-6676.2015.00180.x

Lin, Y.-W., & Bratton, S. C. (n.d.). Summary of play therapy meta-analyses findings. Retrieved from http://evidencebasedchildtherapy.com/meta-analysesreviews/

Mancillas, A. (2006). Counseling students' perceptions of counseling effectiveness. In G. R. Walz, J. C. Bleuer, & R. K. Yep (Eds.), *Vistas: Compelling perspectives on counseling 2006* (pp. 191–194). Alexandria, VA: American Counseling Association.

Mullen, J. A., & Rickli, J. M. (2014). *Child-centered play therapy workbook*. Champaign, IL: Research Press.

Olson-Morrison, D. (2017). Integrative play therapy with adults with complex trauma: A developmentally-informed approach. *International Journal of Play Therapy, 26*(3), 172–183. doi:10.1037/pla0000036

Peabody, M. A., & Schaefer, C. E. (2016). Towards semantic clarity in play therapy. *International Journal of Play Therapy, 25*(4), 197–202. doi:10.1037/pla0000025

Perry, B. D. (2006). Applying principles of neurodevelopment to clinical work with mal-treated and traumatized children: the neurosequential model of therapeutics. In N. B. Webb (Ed.), *Working with traumatized youth in child welfare* (pp. 27–52). New York, NY: Guilford Press.

Porges, S. W. (2011). *The polyvagal theory: Neurophysiological foundations of emotions, attach-ment, communication, and self-regulation*. New York, NY: W W Norton & Co.

Porges, S. W. (2015). Play as neural exercise: insights from the Polyvagal Theory. In D. Pearce-McCall (Ed.), *The power of play for mind brain health* (pp. 3–7). Available from http://mindgains.org/

Ray, D. C. (2011). *Advanced play therapy: Essential conditions, knowledge and skills for child practice*. New York: Routledge.

Ray, D. C., Armstrong, S. A., Balkin, R. S., & Jayne, K. M. (2015). Child-centered play ther-apy in the schools: Review and meta-analysis. *Psychology in the Schools, 52*(2), 107–123. doi:10.1002/pits.21798

Rogers, C. (1980). *A way of being*. New York: Houghton Mifflin Company.

Siegel, D. J. (2010). *The mindful therapist: A clinician's guide to mindsight and neural integra-tion*. New York, NY: W W Norton & Co.

van der Kolk, B. A. (2014). *The body keeps the score: Brain, mind, and body in the healing of trauma*. New York, NY: Viking.

Wells, H. G. (2017). *Little wars & floor games*. Scotts Valley, CA: CreateSpace Independent Publishing Platform.

Wheeler, N., & Dillman Taylor, D. (2016). Integrating interpersonal neurobiology with play therapy. *International Journal of Play Therapy, 25*(1), 24–34. doi:10.1037/pla0000018

Part I

Creative Play Therapy and Core Needs

Creative Play Therapy is an adaptation of play therapy for older clients. With children, the therapist provides a playroom with carefully selected toys to facilitate nurturing, aggressive, real life and creative expression (Landreth, 2012), but with Creative Play Therapy, the therapist expands the creative category of "toys" (perhaps with a more professional grade of materials) to provide expressive arts tools for all forms of expression from an adult perspective. The creative expression is supplemented with talk therapy, not the other way around. Then, the therapist facilitates the stages of Creative Play Therapy while uncovering core needs, considering those needs within the context of development, taking into account any trauma during development along with current developmental stages.

This section will set the context for Creative Play Therapy, explain seven kinds of expressive arts and the basic materials needed, discuss how to use traditional talk therapy to supplement creative work, describe core needs and how to identify them, and review developmental models. These are the five areas of knowledge that inform the Creative Play Therapy: play therapy, expressive arts, talk therapy, core needs and development. See Figure 0.1.

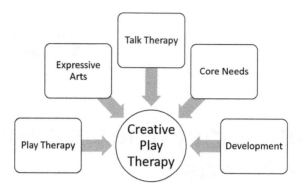

Figure 0.1 Knowledge Blocks That Inform Creative Play Therapy

References

Landreth, G. L. (2012). *Play therapy: The art of the relationship* (3rd ed.) New York: Routledge.

What Is Creative Play Therapy?

1

People of all ages benefit from safe, accepting environments to risk expressing thoughts, feelings, and behaviors (Breen & Daigneault, 1998). Although play therapy has traditionally been a treatment for children, it can also be effective with adolescents and adults. In Creative Play Therapy, we use expressive arts instead of toys, add prompts strategically during some stages of the process, and focus the therapeutic work on core needs. While still grounded in client-centered theory, it is, at times, more directive. This chapter will provide an overview.

Play Therapy with Adolescents and Adults

Play therapy works with adolescents, especially when expressive arts replace more juvenile toys. For adolescents who may have limited experiences of empathy or disrupted early relationships, play therapy provides an opportunity to experience a secure, close relationship through a therapeutic alliance characterized by empathy, not being judged and permissiveness (Green et al., 2013). Adolescents naturally gravitate toward expressive arts seeking self-expression, turning to arts-based methods of coping, such as reaching for a journal, playing a musical instrument, or painting (Perryman et al., 2015). Like child play therapy, play therapy with adolescents incorporates natural forms of expression that are developmentally appropriate.

Adolescents internalize safety and security through the psychologically safe therapeutic relationship as they express raw, honest emotions directly or symbolically without judgment or being asked to change parts of themselves that others may see as unacceptable or undesirable (Green et al., 2013). They respond well to play therapy as they develop self-awareness and individual identity, but adolescent play is based more in reality than fantasy and is characterized by logic, rules, and structure (Breen & Daigneault, 1998). Understanding this desire for logic, rules and structure, Creative Play Therapy incorporates prompts to help build trust and safety.

Play therapy can be an effective treatment for adults who experienced early childhood trauma by addressing fundamental core developmental deficits (Olson-Morrison, 2017). It also has been used to work with child alter personalities, in clients with multiple personality disorder, now known as Dissociative Identity Disorder (Klein & Landreth, 1993), and adults with developmental disabilities (Demanchick et al., 2003). But play therapy can also be used with the general adult population. Greenwald (1967) even advocated for play therapy for clients over 21 more than 50 years ago.

While rigorous research studies provide evidence of large beneficial effects from a variety of psychotherapies that work with children, adults and older adults (APA, 2012), not all who seek services are finding these benefits. Among adults who received some type of mental health service in the previous year, 5.9 million (nearly 20%) reported an unmet need for mental health care according to the American Counseling Association (ACA, 2011). That means that millions of people who are accessing services are not finding relief. They need something more; something that goes deeper; something that heals.

The cost of not helping those with mental illness is staggering. In the United States alone, the estimated cost is $63 billion in lost productivity, $12 billion in mortality costs, and $4 billion in in productivity costs for those who are incarcerated and those who provide family care – for a grand total cost of a whopping $79 billion *per year* (ACA, 2011). Traditional talk therapy has helped many people, but only using a verbal approach misses the opportunity to provide treatment using both hemispheres of the brain, one that physiologically facilitates healing and generates new neuron growth.

The Definition of Play Therapy

Natural play serves six important purposes: fun, symbolic expression, catharsis, social development, mastery, and releasing energy (Ray, 2011). When natural play is combined with therapeutic objectives, it is often called play therapy, but credentialed play therapists would argue that adding toys or playful activities to therapy does not necessarily mean that it is play therapy.

The Association for Play Therapy, a professional organization with more than 7,100 members (APT, 2019b) defines play therapy with the following criteria (APT, 2019a):

> Play Therapy is defined by the Association for Play Therapy as, 'the systematic use of a theoretical model to establish an interpersonal process wherein trained Play Therapists use the therapeutic powers of play to help clients prevent or resolve psychosocial difficulties and achieve optimal growth and development.'
>
> www.a4pt.org

1. Play therapy is systematic.
2. It follows a theoretical model.
3. The theory establishes an interpersonal process.
4. Trained play therapists use the therapeutic powers of play.
5. The goal is to help clients prevent or resolve psychosocial difficulties and achieve optimal growth and development.

What is notably missing from the definition of play therapy (APT, 2019a) is that it is only applicable to work with children. Although mostly used for children, the benefits of this treatment modality go well beyond the limits of age. However, it is a systematic approach that includes four elements: a theoretical model, an interpersonal process, therapeutic powers of play, and optimal growth and development. Creative Play Therapy meets these four criteria. NOTE: You may not align exactly with the systematic approach outlined below, and that is fine. Be authentic to your own training and beliefs.

- *Theoretical Model.* Theory provides a broad conceptual framework, a consistent system to view, assess and communicate with clients (Peabody & Schaefer, 2016). Creative Play Therapy is based upon the client-centered approach developed by Carl Rogers, but we encourage practitioners to expand from there. Philosophically, this means that we are oriented to believe the following, which is client-centered theory filtered through the Creative Play Therapy treatment modality:
  - Clients have inherent growth potential, and they are autonomous and direct their process (but with scaffolding from the therapist).
  - The environment is permissive for freedom and responsibility.
  - Reflective listening is THE technique, but we supplement it with skills, education and professional intuition.

- Through this theoretical lens, the focus is on the present with an understanding that the present is shaped by the past and leads to the future.
- Feelings occur before thoughts and behavior, often below awareness. However, thoughts can influence feelings (and vice versa), and both precede behavior, so by changing them, you change behaviors.
- Finally, we are strongly shaped, but not determined by our culture.
- *Interpersonal Process.* The relationship between the therapist and client is seen as critically important to Creative Play Therapy. In other words, the relationship is the therapy, and the three core conditions of genuineness, unconditional positive regard, and empathic understanding facilitate the relationship (C. Rogers, 1980). The therapeutic relationship is more valuable than any intervention used in play therapy, and it improves the quality of a client's future relationships (Green et al., 2013).
- *Therapeutic powers of play.* Creative Play Therapy uses play through the expressive arts as a means for clients to communicate what they are afraid, unwilling or unable to say. Sometimes, play is accomplished through metaphors, which are used in all cultural groups and may help especially with negative emotions that are too painful to express directly (Gladding, 2016). The tools used are expressive arts supplies (preferably professional grade) to externalize what is happening internally for the client. Play through the expressive arts facilitates communication, fosters emotional wellness, enhances social relationships, and increases personal strengths (Drewes & Schaefer, 2016)
- *Optimal growth and development.* Creative Play Therapy offers a treatment modality of healing. The client's core needs are identified (safety and security, empowerment and control, inner value, and relationship needs), including the specific themes for each client. Most mental diagnoses are viewed as symptoms, and they are resolved by gaining a fuller understanding of the core need at the root of the problem.

The Association for Play Therapy (APT, n.d.) is the only professional organization that provides the Registered Play Therapist and Registered Play Therapist Supervisor credentials. (They also offer a school-based option.) It is important to reiterate that those using Creative Play Therapy and other play therapy approaches should be professionally trained both in their given fields and in play therapy. Visit the APT website for specific requirements for credentialing at www.a4pt.org.

What Are Expressive Arts?

Natalie Rogers wrote that creative activities are therapeutic and therapy is a creative process (N. Rogers, 2013). The expressive arts provide a way for clients to experience the paradox of the play being real and not real at the same time (Etzi, 2004). Developmentally, adolescents are prone to egocentric thinking, but expressive arts help them look outside themselves (Perryman et al., 2015). They provide a way for both adolescents and adults to externalize what is happening internally.

In this book, we will use the blanket term of expressive arts to include seven categories. This is not intended to be an exhaustive list, but a sufficient list for you to consider how to integrate a few into your work with clients. Chapter 2 will expand the descriptions of each one and materials to include. Expressive Arts include the following:

- Art
- Drama
- Dance and Movement
- Music
- Photography
- Sand
- Writing

Expressive arts are the 'toys' when working with adolescents and adults. They become the tools for the client to communicate what is often difficult to capture with words alone. They allow clients to warm up, be expressive, nurture themselves, and find meaning.

How Does Creative Play Therapy Work?

The remainder of the book will provide details and examples, but here is a quick summary of the Creative Play Therapy process and the stages of therapy. Use this as a guide, not a protocol, since each client will be different. As you gain experience, you will become more comfortable with the fluidity of the process, but the figures will help you as you are learning.

The therapeutic process is ongoing and cyclical. First, create a safe environment for clients. Second, prompt clients to externalize an aspect of their

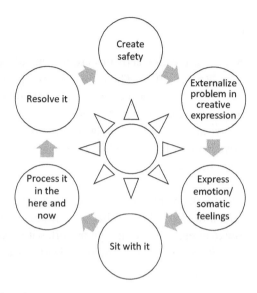

Figure 1.1 The Therapeutic Process

internal worlds utilizing some form of creative expression. Next, allow clients to feel the depth of emotion and physical sensation. Then, patiently sit with it, not rushing to alleviate discomfort, but providing acceptance for what is. After that, process the creation and feeling in the here and now, which leads to resolution. Repeat this process throughout the time you work together. At times, you will complete the cycle all in one session, but other times, you will spend most of your time on one spot of the process. See Figure 1.1.

While the process in Figure 1.1 is how you do Creative Play Therapy, the stages are a linear depiction of what happens as you move through the process. There are seven distinct stages of Creative Play Therapy, but in the process, you may cycle through stages two to six multiple times. The stages begin with a warm up, but creating safety is a continuous part of the process. The second stage is creation, externalizing the client's experience. The next stages are emotional and somatic expression, which are separate stages, but the client may express more intensity with one or the other. The fifth stage is meaning-making, something that adults, especially, seek. The sixth stage is healing, the resolution of the problem, or an aspect of the problem. Finally, as your work together concludes, the last stage is ending.

This provides an overview of how Creative Play Therapy works. What is not included in Figure 1.2 is the depth of work that this process facilitates. Though we have tried to convey both the therapeutic process and the stages as simply as possible to make it easier to learn, Creative Play Therapy is not simple.

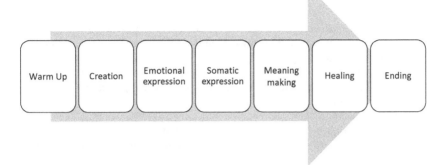

Figure 1.2   The Seven Stages of Creative Play Therapy

Creative Application: Mark Up Your Book

This book is about Creative Play Therapy, so the first application we recommend is for you to be creative in your learning. You bought this book, and we want you to make it as useful to your learning as possible. Use color, drawings and shapes to mark the book while reading it. Feel free to highlight, underline and jot notes in the margins, but also experiment with visual doodles while you digest the material, testing different mediums and adding symbols that help you visually remember the content.

Summary

Play therapy, although developed and used primarily with children, is also an effective treatment with adolescents and adults. Creative Play Therapy meets the criteria for the definition of play therapy. It is the systematic use of a theoretical model to establish an interpersonal process where trained Play Therapists use the therapeutic powers of play to help clients prevent or resolve psychosocial difficulties and achieve optimal growth and development (APT, 2019a). Using expressive arts provides a creative way to play that is both comfortable and communicative for adolescents and adults. It provides a means for clients to externalize what is happening internally, see it from a third person perspective, and test changes. We now turn to learning how to incorporate the expressive arts into Creative Play Therapy.

References

ACA. (2011). *The effectiveness of and need for professional counseling services.* Retrieved from Alexandria, VA. Retrieved from www.counseling.org/docs/public-policy-resources-reports/effectiveness_of_and_need_for_counseling_2011.pdf?sfvrsn=2

APA. (2012). *Recognition of psychotherapy effectiveness.* Retrieved from https://search.ebscohost.com/login.aspx?direct=true&AuthType=sso&db=psyh&AN=2013-30990-003&site=ehost-live&custid=s8863735

APT. (2019a). *Guidelines.* Retrieved from www.a4pt.org/page/ClarifyingUseofPT

APT. (2019b). *Homepage.* Retrieved from www.a4pt.org/default.aspx

APT. (n.d.). *Play therapy credentials.* Retrieved from www.a4pt.org/page/Credentials Homepage

Breen, D. T., & Daigneault, S. D. (1998). The use of play therapy with adolescents in high school. *International Journal of Play Therapy, 7*(1), 25–47. doi:10.1037/h0089417

Demanchick, S. P., Cochran, N. H., & Cochran, J. L. (2003). Person-centered play therapy for adults with developmental disabilities. *International Journal of Play Therapy, 12*(1), 47–65. doi:10.1037/h0088871

Drewes, A. A., & Schaefer, C. E. (2016). The therapeutic powers of play. In K. J. O'Connor, C. E. Schaefer, & L. D. Braverman (Eds.), *Handbook of play therapy* (2nd ed., pp. 35–60). Hoboken, NJ: John Wiley & Sons Inc.

Etzi, J. (2004). Analysis of play. *The Humanistic Psychologist, 32*(Summer), 239–256.

Gladding, S. (2016). *The creative arts in counseling* (5th ed.) Alexandria, VA: American Counseling Association.

Green, E. J., Myrick, A. C., & Crenshaw, D. A. (2013). Toward secure attachment in adolescent relational development: Advancements from sandplay and expressive play-based interventions. *International Journal of Play Therapy, 22*(2), 90–102. doi:10.1037/a0032323

Greenwald, H. (1967). Play therapy for children over twenty-one. *Psychotherapy: Theory, Research & Practice, 4*(1), 44–46. doi:10.1037/h0087932

Klein, J. W., & Landreth, G. L. (1993). Play therapy with multiple personality disorder clients. *International Journal of Play Therapy, 2*(1), 1–14. doi:10.1037/h0089059

Olson-Morrison, D. (2017). Integrative play therapy with adults with complex trauma: A developmentally-informed approach. *International Journal of Play Therapy, 26*(3), 172–183. doi:10.1037/pla0000036

Peabody, M. A., & Schaefer, C. E. (2016). Towards semantic clarity in play therapy. *International Journal of Play Therapy, 25*(4), 197–202. doi:10.1037/pla0000025

Perryman, K. L., Moss, R., & Cochran, K. (2015). Child-centered expressive arts and play therapy: School groups for at-risk adolescent girls. *International Journal of Play Therapy, 24*(4), 205–220. doi:10.1037/a0039764

Ray, D. C. (2011). *Advanced play therapy: Essential conditions, knowledge and skills for child practice.* New York: Routledge.

Rogers, C. (1980). *A way of being.* New York: Houghton Mifflin Company.

Rogers, N. (2013). Person-centred expressive arts therapy: Connecting body, mind and spirit. In M. Cooper, M. O'Hara, P. F. Schmid, A. C. Bohart, M. Cooper, M. O'Hara, P. F. Schmid, & A. C. Bohart (Eds.), *The handbook of person-centred psychotherapy and counselling* (2nd ed., pp. 237–247). New York: Palgrave Macmillan.

What Materials Are Needed for Creative Play Therapy?

2

With an understanding of the field of play therapy, how do you adapt the language of play in a way that is useful with adolescents and adults? The answer is to expand the creative category of toys, use adult-grade materials (this is debatable, but you do want to avoid a juvenile environment), and create a safe space for the client to externalize what is happening internally to process the creation. This chapter will introduce seven expressive arts from which to choose, along with a supply list for each. Since each of the expressive arts is a distinct professional field, this chapter provides a short summary, and you are encouraged to seek further training and knowledge in the ones that appeal to you.

Externalizing Internal Emotions

In Creative Play Therapy, the basic purpose is to facilitate the process for clients to externalize their internal emotions, sometimes a complex tangle of emotions. Clients often censor what they choose to say, intentionally or not, but in creating a physical product, what we call the creation, clients express the nuances of what they experience, understand, and believe in a concrete form that you both can see, touch, hear and then change. It is more revealing to both of you. It does not really matter if that physical creation is an art collage, a sand tray, or a monologue. It could be a photograph, a poem or a song. What matters is that whatever clients create communicates the personal experience of their world to you. After the physical creation is constructed, then you can both see it (or hear it) and make changes, which then translate into unseen changes in perception and beliefs about what may be possible. The expressive art, whatever that may be, is simply a vehicle for external-izing the core need and creating internal changes for the client. Emotions are complex, so creative play therapy simplifies the ability to communicate them with expressive arts.

For example, a client may show a relationship with her partner by using a small kitten to represent herself and a proportionally much larger lion to represent her partner. She may do this with figures in a sand tray, through a sketch drawing, or by choosing digital images from the internet to show you. The creation itself is less important than what it communicates, which in this case could be something around a lack of power in the relationship. The bigger figure usually represents more power, although it may not be physi-cal strength that your client is communicating. This is where the nuances of the communication become important. The client would be communicating something different if she chose a kitten sitting pretty with a smirk expression rather than a kitten balled up to protect herself. As she shows you and then explains to you how she sees that relationship, you use reflections and ques-tions to increase understanding for you both.

Below is an example of how a counselor would use Creative Play Therapy in the scenario above, where the client has shown you the smirking kitten representing herself and the large lion for her partner.

Client:	That's it. That's our relationship.
Therapist:	That shows me your relationship with your partner.
Client:	Yeah. I'm the kitten and my partner is the lion.
Therapist:	The lion seems a lot bigger than the kitten.
Client:	For sure. The lion thinks it could squash the kitten, but the kitten has a secret.
Therapist:	Oh she does? What is the kitten's secret?
Client:	The kitten has that smirk because she knows that the lion is really scared and just blowing steam. The lion yells a lot, but wouldn't really hurt the kitten. [Lowers her voice] But some-times the lion threatens to leave. As long as the kitten keeps the lion from being so scared, it's okay.

In this short exchange, the client has shown the counselor that the client's partner wields the power in the relationship because of the threats to end the relationship. She has also clarified that she is not in physical danger, but the emotional risk is great, so great that admitting it must be whispered. Her role in the relationship, according to her, is to alleviate her partner's fears (we do not yet know what those are), especially when the partner is "blowing steam."

Therapist:	I wonder what would happen if the kitten let the lion stay scared.
Client:	Oh, the kitten couldn't do that.
Therapist:	The kitten could NOT do that.
Client:	No, the lion would really yell then.
Therapist:	Before this, the lion was just sort of yelling.
Client:	Right. The lion was yelling, but not really doing anything about it. If the lion stayed scared, it would move over here ... or actually, way over there. [Moves the lion figure to an end table as far away as the client's arm can stretch.]
Therapist:	So, if the kitten lets the lion stay scared, the lion would move way over there. What about the kitten?
Client:	[pushes kitten over] The kitten would die.

In a very short amount of time, the client has expressed a lot of information. She has communicated that for her, not filling her role of pacifying her partner's fears is not an option. "The kitten couldn't do that." If she did, she believes that her partner would leave, and that leaving would likely be permanent. If that happened, it would overwhelm the client (pushing the kitten over) resulting in a significant ending. When she says, "The kitten would die" it could mean that she would consider suicide *(and this should be properly assessed)*, but it also could be more symbolic. Maybe the death of the relationship would mean losing her identity or purpose. Be cautious about interpreting until the client has told you her meaning for the objects, but also be willing to ask direct questions to assess for suicidality.

What is important to recognize in this scenario is that the client sees it as impossible at this point to not fulfill her role with her partner because the consequences of not doing so are too great. Although the therapist does not yet know what triggers the partner's fears, exactly how the client tries to alleviate those fears, or why the end of the relationship would be so devastating, what the therapist does understand is that this is how the client perceives her relationship. True empathy is understanding the client's world from the client's perspective.

If the client cannot make a change in the creative scene, then the client cannot make that change yet in real life. Therefore, the work with the client should not be around trying to 'get' her to make a behavior change. The work is around understanding the deeper level emotion that prevents change.

Therapist:	The kitten would die if the lion left?
Client:	Who else would love the kitten?
Therapist:	The kitten is unlovable without the lion.
Client:	[begins to cry]

This gets to the core need that is preventing change, and the therapist knows it because of the emotional response without words. The client believes that without her partner, she cannot be loved. Therefore, she is willing to do whatever it takes to keep her partner from leaving, even if it turns the relationship into something that is unhealthy or even toxic. By addressing the core need of her capacity to be loved, it changes possibilities for the client. This informs the future work with the client. In other words, as the client is able to articulate that she fears not being loved, she may reframe that fear, recognize that is untruthful, or identify that her behaviors are a result of those fears. Perhaps she is able to change her response when her partner yells out of fear, and they develop healthier communication. Perhaps she stops feeling the desire to be responsible for her partner's emotions, and while the situation does not change, she has. Or, perhaps what the client is afraid will happen does, and her partner leaves the relationship, but even then, it does not mean that the client is incapable of being loved. The focus of creative play therapy is facilitating that inner change, not working towards a specific outcome. Trust that, given a safe therapeutic relationship, the client will be self-directing. Understanding the core need to be loved and how this client tries to fulfil that need is more global than easing an argument with her partner. While the client has not yet mentioned other relationships, it is likely that this fear of not having her need for love met also impacts those.

The client could have expressed her perception of her relationship with stick figures, drum beats, or geometric shapes. The therapist is seeking to understand what she is communicating, so the kind of expressive tools are based on professional preference. There is not one correct way to do this. Keeping that in mind, the remainder of the chapter will help you with the specific tools that will help clients express deep emotions.

Practical Things to Consider

Before listing some basic supplies that will be helpful for this creative therapeutic work, it is important to consider where you practice and your own
personal preferences. These will inform the creative tools that you select to
include in your therapeutic space. Thoughtful consideration on the front end
may reduce problems later. Also, keep in mind that you will not use all of the
expressive arts listed. Instead, select only two or three so clients have options,
but keep in mind that too many options become overwhelming.

Know Your Setting Limitations

Where do you work with clients?

If you have your own office space and complete freedom to set up that
space, then most of the limitations for you will come from personal preferences. You can choose as many or as few supplies as you feel comfortable
providing, and you can display or organize them in whatever way appeals to
you and the populations with which you work. However, if you share space,
travel to clients or work in a setting with rules (clearly stated or not) about
furniture placement and messes, then you will need to take that into consideration. You may limit messier supplies like paint and water if you share space
with others who would be irritated with accidental spills. Or, you might not
carry heavier supplies like sand if you are traveling.

Know Yourself

If you are continually thinking about how to hand your client a wet wipe to
clean her hands every time she chooses to use pastels, then that distraction
may make it more difficult to be present with your client. If so, do not offer
pastels in your work. If the scraping sound of miniatures being pushed into
the sand grates on your nerves, do not use the sand tray. (You could still use
miniatures without sand.) If you have formal training in music and irregular
uses of instruments bother you, then enjoy music as a hobby, not as part of
your vocation. You do not need to use every kind of creative medium or
every supply possible for each medium. In fact, that might be chaotic for clients. Part of being genuine with clients is recognizing your pet peeves, preferences, and personality. Also recognize that your comfort level with messes

and alternative use of creative media will likely change as you gain experience and learn from your clients. You will be spending most of your working hours in this space, so it should be comfortable for both you and your clients.

> ## Questions to Consider
>
> What kind of clients do you see?
>
> How much storage space do you have available for supplies?
>
> Is it open storage or closed cabinets?
>
> Do you need your supplies to travel with you?
>
> Which expressive arts are highly interesting to you?
>
> Which expressive arts do you have training in using?
>
> What expressive arts supplies do you already use in your work?
>
> What are your personal preferences for visual clutter?
>
> What is your personal tolerance for noise?
>
> What is your personal tolerance for water, paint, sand, and other messes?
>
> What constraints on messes and noise come from your setting?
>
> What kind of impact do the expressive arts supplies in your office have on your clients?

Start with One or Two Expressive Options

If you are just beginning to use creative expression in your helping work, then start with one or two options. Too much stuff in your office may be overwhelming for clients, as are too many choices. In trying to provide everything a client might need, you will actually make it more difficult for them to make choices and do the therapeutic work. You can always add items later, so starting simply allows you to test out an expressive art with your clients.

When I, Dr. Denis', began using expressive arts in my work, I started with art because I already had those basic supplies available in my school counseling office. I had blank copy paper in the printer and a supply of markers and crayons. I would offer those to clients with an open prompt to draw whatever they liked while we got to know each other. Then, I would usually ask them to draw their family, the people and pets that live in their home. Later, I added writing techniques. I did not use music, photography or sand techniques at all in those early years. Those came later, and the same will be true as you set up your space. You probably have one or two areas of expressive arts that already appeal to you, or maybe that you already have used. Start there, and add others as your knowledge and training expand.

Creative Play Therapy Toys

Garry Landreth (2012), is famous for saying, "Toys are used like words by children, and play is their language" (p. 12). The same is true as we translate this work to adolescents and adults. The toys, or expressive arts supplies, will provide the tools to communicate more than words, and the play, or creative expression, will be the language for that communication. In Landreth's child-centered play therapy approach, he conceptualized four categories of toys: nurturing, aggressive release, real life, and creative. In Creative Play Therapy, the toys all come from the creative category, though they may serve the purpose of the other categories. See Figure 2.1.

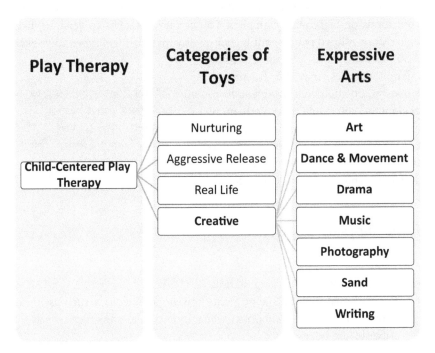

Figure 2.1   How Expressive Arts Are Part of Play Therapy

The remainder of this book will explore how to use the treatment modality of play therapy with adults by using the expressive arts as the tools for the client to communicate. The next section will outline some basic supplies for each of the expressive arts. The lists below are not exhaustive, but intended to give you a starting guide. Although they will be discussed separately, you might want to combine arts. Natalie Rogers combined movement, art, writing and sound into what she called the creative connection (N. Rogers, 2013).

Art

Art has been used since primitive times to symbolically express feelings and to communicate (Breen & Daigneault, 1998). Art therapy incorporates all techniques from the visual arts: drawing, sketching, acrylic painting, watercolor, collage, pastels, finger painting, etc. It includes the fine arts as well as folk arts, crafts such as pottery, quilting, and wood crafts with traditional roots (Glăveanu, 2013). Consider the mediums with which you are already comfortable and have experience and select supplies accordingly. You do not need every supply for every art medium. Instead, select a few areas and concentrate your funds on high quality supplies. You can use inexpensive versions, like dollar store colored pencils, but higher quality materials feel more adult-like. Also, if clients have art training, using inferior supplies may be frustrating. However, do not let cost keep you from beginning. You could start with more inexpensive options and then upgrade later when you have a better understanding of what your clients tend to use and prefer and what you like to offer.

> Visit http://arttherapy.org to learn more about training and credentialing in art therapy from the American Art Therapy Association.

Basic Supplies

- Paper
- Writing/coloring/marking utensils
- Foundational materials appropriate for the art medium such as loose paper, canvases, sketchbooks, watercolor paper, construction paper, paper plates, boxes, etc.

- Art mediums like acrylic paint, watercolor, pastels, colored pencils, colored markers, charcoals, clay, etc.
- Art materials like brushes, sponges, water containers, pallets, glue, paint trays, easel, scissors, yarn, beads, crepe paper, crafting supplies, erasers, pottery shaping sticks, etc.
- Cleaning materials such as soap and water, hand wipes, paper towels, etc.

Drama

Drama includes anything theatrical, and the techniques incorporate acting, monologues, group interaction, puppets or marionettes, cinema, costumes and props, among others. Theatrical techniques may incorporate groups or be used with individuals. Creative dramatics allows clients to try out new roles, learn to understand other perspectives, hone problem solving skills, increase a sense of belonging, and confront the self that is, the self that one fears, and the self one wishes to be (Breen & Daigneault, 1998). The client may be the actor (a first-person perspective) or the director (a third-person perspective). Props offer tremendous possibilities, but they may also be imaginary. Translating the testimony of personal trauma history into artistic language makes the witnessing active, allowing the client to reconstruct self-identity, and adds nonverbal interpersonal communication, facial expression, gestures, pauses, and vocal intonations (Peleg, Lev-Wiesel, & Yaniv, 2014). Gladding even noted that drama and counseling have seven parallels (Gladding, 2016):

1. Clients learn to experience a range of emotions and express them appropriately.
2. Both counseling and drama rely on the impact of timing.
3. Dramatic movement is a natural part of the process.
4. Life difficulties are reflected through dramatic means.
5. Clients become more attuned to their feelings and integrate all parts of themselves in a holistic way.
6. Participants gain insight by identifying with certain expressions.
7. Both are relationship oriented and rely on space for creative spontaneity.

Visit www.nadta.org/education-and-credentialing.html to learn more about certification as a registered drama therapist from the North American Drama Therapy Association.

Basic Supplies

- Cast – people, figures, family sets, puppets/marionettes
- Props – furniture, household items, prop lesson items, other props
- Costumes – capes, clothes, boots, hats, character costumes
- Sets – diorama, stage sets, realistic doll house, backdrops
- Scripts – written by client or others

Dance and Movement

These techniques use many forms of body movement: dance, exercise, martial arts, self-defense, yoga, walking, treadmill, boxing, and stillness. Because they may require more space than a typical office, these may take place in outdoor or open settings, so staying aware of confidentiality is essential. When people feel chronic emotions, such as anger or fear, they experience physical ailments and chronic pain from muscle tension, and without awareness of body needs, you cannot care for the body (van der Kolk, 2014). Movement can be powerful to incorporate in therapeutic work because it utilizes both sides of the body and the brain.

> Visit www.adta.org to learn more about the requirements to becoming a registered dance and movement therapist from the American Dance Therapy Association.

Basic Supplies

- Indoor space that is large enough for movement
- Outdoor spaces
- Sporting goods – yoga mats, boxing gloves, balls *of various sizes*, resistance bands, weighted blankets, etc.
- Exercise machines
- First aid kit.

Music

Music can be incorporated as background sound or as the creative expression, from beats to melodies to song writing. Music can be generated by the client or incorporated by listening to playlists or specifically selected music. Like many of the expressive arts, music can be combined with other expressive arts, such as writing, or layered with other expressive arts, such as listening to meaningful song while creating a sand tray.

Visit www.musictherapy.org/about/requirements/ to learn more about certification through the American Music Therapy Association.

Basic Supplies

- Electronics – radio, phone, computer, tablet, speakers, etc.
- Instruments – guitar, keyboard, bongos, synthesizer, xylophone, tambourine, bells, etc.
- Editing Software – Garage Band, Audacity or other mixing software
- Writing materials – blank paper or sheet music, writing instruments
- Internet access – to look up songs and lyrics.

Photography

Photography techniques can use physical or digital photographs, and you now have more options than ever. Photographic therapy is usually classified under art therapy, so it can easily be incorporated with other visual arts. However, since digital photography is so easily and inexpensively accessible, we have chosen to categorize photography separately from art. Physical photos can be cut and shaped into a collage or arranged in a timeline, but this can also be arranged and edited electronically with digital photos. Clients can take pictures on their phones anywhere and as often as needed to show you their perception of their world or diagnosis. Alternately, they can find images online that capture how they feel. With easily accessible software, digital images can be manipulated to distort or change the photo. This expressive art could also include videos.

To learn more about training and credentialing in art and photo therapy visit http://phototherapy-centre.com

Basic Supplies

- Photo or video capturing tools – camera, phone, or other device
- Photos – print or digital

- Photo editing – software, photo pens, scissors
- Photo collecting/collaging – timelines, collages, other ways to assemble photos
- Scrapbooking supplies.

Sand

The differences between sand tray and sand play exceed the scope of this book, but both will require further training to ethically use these techniques. The general idea is that sand provides an earthy medium for clients to create or project their world. Miniatures offer many three-dimensional possibilities for clients to use as tools, and they can be quickly and easily moved around.

Sand Play has an extensive credentialing process, including personal work.

Learn more at: www.sandplay.org/membership/certified-member

As of this printing, there is no national credentialing for sand tray.

Basic Supplies

- Sand – plain, colored, kinetic
- Sand tray – rectangular, other shapes
- Tools – smoothing, raking, scooping
- Miniatures – people, animals, nature objects, barriers, bridges, elements (water, fire), escape vehicles, metaphoric representations, sacred symbols, mythical creatures, soldiers, weapons etc.

Writing

Writing techniques can be done digitally or with physical paper. Digital is often more convenient, especially for homework, but writing by hand may feel more organic and accessible. Digital may seem more private, since it can be password protected, but handwritten prose can curl around the page. The work done is more important than the medium chosen. You might even strategically mix the two forms.

Basic Supplies

- Computer or device
- Thesaurus and rhyming dictionary
- Paper – different textures, colors, and sizes
- Writing implements – different kinds
- Journal or notebook
- Magnetic words
- Dry erase board and markers / chalkboard and chalk.

Creative Application

Consider your ideal therapeutic space. Create a sketch of what you would like it to look like. How will the furniture be arranged? What supplies would you like to have, and how will you store them? What color scheme would you like? How will you incorporate sound? What material would the floor be? What would you like to convey from the environmental space?

You might want to use an online program like Roomstyler to help.

References

Breen, D. T., & Daigneault, S. D. (1998). The use of play therapy with adolescents in high school. *International Journal of Play Therapy*, 7(1), 25–47. doi:10.1037/h0089417

Gladding, S. (2016). *The creative arts in counseling* (5th ed.) Alexandria, VA: American Counseling Association.

Glăveanu, V. P. (2013). Creativity and folk art: A study of creative action in traditional craft. *Psychology of Aesthetics, Creativity, and the Arts*, 7(2), 140–154. https://doi.org/10.1037/a0029318.supp

Landreth, G. L. (2012). *Play therapy: The art of the relationship* (3rd ed.) New York: Routledge.

Peleg, M., Lev-Wiesel, R., & Yaniv, D. (2014). Reconstruction of self-identity of Holocaust child survivors who participated in "Testimony Theater." *Psychological Trauma: Theory, Research, Practice, and Policy*, 6(4), 411–419. https://doi.org/10.1037/a0033834

Rogers, N. (2013). Person-centred expressive arts therapy: Connecting body, mind and spirit. In M. Cooper, M. O'Hara, P. F. Schmid, A. C. Bohart, M. Cooper, M. O'Hara, P. F. Schmid, & A. C. Bohart (Eds.), *The handbook of person-centred psychotherapy and counselling* (2nd ed., pp. 237–247). New York: Palgrave Macmillan.

van der Kolk, B. A. (2014). *The body keeps the score: Brain, mind, and body in the healing of trauma*. London: Viking Penguin.

Why Is Talking Only Part of the Process? 3

Students enrolled in programs in the helping professions take classes to develop listening and questioning skills. A skill is simply the ability to apply knowledge effectively and readily in practice (Peabody & Schaefer, 2016). Listening and questioning skills are predicated on the idea that the client will be talking. In the class, students learn how to ask open-ended questions and respond in ways that "get the client talking." These are invaluable courses when working with hurting people, and we teach them in our program, too. In fact, the end of this chapter will address active listening and reflective responding, and the examples will be in the context of conversation.

Sometimes, though, client issues are so complex that using words to communicate the experience is inadequate. Van der Kolk (2014), in the groundbreaking book *The Body Keeps the Score* wrote (p. 178):

> When something terrifying happens, like seeing a child or a friend get hurt in an accident, we will retain an intense and fairly accurate memory of the event for a long time... the more adrenalin you secrete, the more precise your memory will be, but that is true only up to a certain point. Confronted with horror – especially the horror of "inescapable shock" – the system becomes overwhelmed and breaks down.

Green et al. (2013) described Jungian Play Therapy (JPT) as "an alternative to traditional talk therapy...that facilitates healing through the expression of one's subconscious images, metaphors and symbols based on analytic psychology. The language of JPT is visual rather than verbal" (p. 161). The authors explain that healing is not accomplished through techniques, but through the personal self-healing archetype that emerges within the context of a safe therapeutic relationship. Although we use different language and have different training, this is the process that happens in Creative Play Therapy as well.

Part 2 of the book will walk you through the seven phases of Creative Play Therapy, and some of those phases will be mostly silence, depending on the client. This chapter outlines how to use verbal conversation to supplement the work that is being done nonverbally. Using expressive arts provides alternative options for communication, providing information that might have remained unknown, because the art allows for unconscious feelings or unknown stories to surface and be processed at the client's pace (Perryman et al., 2015). This is quite different from most approaches. The primary therapist role in Creative Play Therapy is presence, not conversation. Although the healing work is often happening without words, knowing how to listen and use words to reflect that work back to the client are essential skills in Creative Play Therapy.

Traditional Talk Therapy

Most adolescents and adults, unlike children, usually expect to talk and are comfortable with verbally expressing themselves. Rarely are adult clients mute or physically incapable of speech, although those examples are great times to use Creative Play Therapy. More often, clients will use words to talk circles around the issue without really doing the needed therapeutic work. While talking about problems may be helpful, it is not always the best way to deep, healing work.

Talk therapy is *the* approach that is taught in counseling, psychology, social work, marriage and family therapy and other graduate programs. Whether you philosophically believe the problem can be changed through thoughts, emotions or actions, dialoging with the client is the standard for assessing how the client perceives his or her world and understanding what has gone wrong. Undoubtedly, this approach has helped thousands of people, but Creative Play Therapy work is deeper than simply helping. Creative Play Therapy moves beyond helping and facilitates healing.

Talk therapy utilizes the analytic left hemisphere of the brain. This is great for problem solving once a problem can be identified and clear steps to resolve the problem can be generated. For example, if a client is in danger of failing classes because of test anxiety (the identified problem), then together you can generate the steps to reduce anxiety physically and cognitively and thus improve test performance. This logical problem-solving process takes place in that left brain, and it can be quite helpful to clients.

However, what if the client is in danger of failing classes because of recurrent nightmares that are causing significant sleep problems? You could use the typically taught problem-solving approach and help the client find some relief. Perhaps you could generate steps to wind down and prepare the body for rest each evening or physically tire the body during the day. Maybe that helps, but it will not heal the client because the underlying reason for the nightmares has not been addressed. For the client, the nightmares serve a purpose, but the client probably does not fully understand what his or her sleeping body is trying to communicate, especially in cases of complex trauma. One of two things will happen if the therapist only uses a talk therapy, problem-solving treatment: 1) it will not reduce the nightmares and the problems will continue, or 2) it will reduce the nightmares, but another equally problematic symptom will develop.

The nightmares are not the problem. They are a symptom of a deeper core need that the nightmares are cuing the client to understand. Typically, they will escalate and become more problematic or other symptoms will also develop and become a constellation of hints about the deeper problem. The discomfort from this is what drives clients to seek help.

Talking has been the best way helpers have known to communicate about problems, but it only goes so far in providing permanent relief, which makes sense since it only uses half of the brain. Using creative play therapy allows the client to use the right hemisphere of the brain, too. This side of the brain thinks in colors, images and emotions, but not words. Therefore, using expressive arts can work very well at accessing this part of the brain, but language will not. When the therapist becomes skilled at facilitating therapeutic work that goes back and forth, using both hemispheres of the brain, true healing begins. Research indicates that physical healing also happens as new neuro pathways develop in the corpus collosum during this process (Cozolino, 2017).

Some clients are highly adept at talking around their problems. Some use this as a strategy to avoid actually doing the therapeutic work. Some feel safer talking, not out of avoidance, but out of fear of digging into the problem. Some talk freely, but do not know how to get deeper to the real issue. Creative Play Therapy offers an alternative and longer lasting solution.

In Creative Play Therapy, clients are able to warm up with traditional talk therapy, and then create a tangible product to show the therapist how they think, feel and act. The beginning uses the left brain, but that creation process accesses the right hemisphere of the brain. Then, as the therapist facilitates meaning making, the client moves back and forth between left brain and right brain, which leads to integrated healing. The architecture of the brain actually changes during play therapy, and the therapist – client relationship positively influences neuron growth (Wheeler & Dillman Taylor, 2016).

Reflective Responses

While facilitating Creative Play Therapy has been described by our students as magical, mind-blowing and awesome, it truly is a learned skill. One of the most fundamental skills to facilitate this process is reflective listening. Reflective responses are how the therapist conveys the four messages of safety (Landreth, 2012), which include: I am here, I hear you, I understand and I care. Reflective listening and responding are the most essential skills in creative play therapy.

Creative Application

The best way to develop the skill of reflection is to practice, practice, practice until it becomes natural. At first, it will seem artificial because it is such a different way of communicating. It usually seems more awkward to you than to the person with whom you are communicating. Try using only reflective responses (no questions) in a conversation with a friend or family member today and see what happens. Try it again with another person and notice what happens this time. Did the person talk more? In more depth? Did the person slip into a contemplative quiet? If you like, ask that person what they noticed after you have practiced reflection for a few minutes. Finally, try just reflecting (without questions) in a conversation with a stranger.

To become skilled at reflective listening and responding, it may be helpful to have the knowledge of exactly what it is and the purpose of using the skill. Below, we outline the types of reflective responses and examples of how to use them. Again, practice is the best way to fully learn the skill.

Active Listening

First, begin by listening to the client. In active listening, the entire focus is on understanding the client's world from the client's perspective, or empathy. You are not thinking about your next question or how to tie what they are saying into treatment goals. Instead, you want to really understand how this person experiences the problem. Active listening is very focused and highly attuned to the client.

This kind of listening also requires being an acute observer. The therapist becomes a keen detective of nonverbal body language as well as verbal communication, noticing any patterns or inconsistencies. Does the client smile while describing tragedy? Does she always lean back to add distance when talking about her sister? Does he cross his arms defensively when talking about his job?

Active listening means balancing being in the moment with the client and being in your head as you analytically sift through the information the client is giving. As a beginner, lean toward being in the moment and noticing while trusting your professionally informed intuition. Then, as your skills develop, you will become better able to switch to your left-brain analysis in the moment. If you start by being in your head, it is much more difficult to be in the moment. See Figure 3.1.

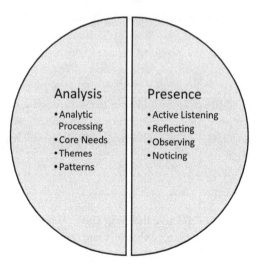

Figure 3.1   The Therapist Mind

Before making any verbal responses, be aware of how you communicate nonverbally to your client.

- Do you have any physical objects (a laptop, clipboard, desk, crossed arms or legs, etc.) between you? These are barriers.
- Are you leaning forward with interest, but not with too much intensity? This conveys a genuine attempt to understand.
- Are you making eye contact that conveys interest? This helps the client feel heard, but not interrogated (one may need to be considerate of cultural differences here).
- Do you nod your head to encourage your client? This gives the client the support to continue.
- Are your nose and knees pointed towards the client? This assures the client that your focus is entirely on him.
- Is your client responding positively to your nonverbal communication? This is valuable feedback for you, for regardless of your intentions, if your communication is not received, you need to work on rapport building.

Really hear your client before responding. Listen with the goal of understanding and communicating back to the client that you understand. Sometimes, you will not understand completely and you will make mistakes, but if clients trust that you are genuinely trying, they usually appreciate your efforts and clarify.

Reflective Responding

After listening to understand, your response can either maintain the depth of the conversation at the current level, move the conversation deeper, or bring it up to a shallower level (see Figure 3.2). All three are needed at different times, but it is important to be purposeful. If the session is ending, then the therapist needs to be able to strategically move the conversation to a more shallow level. However, beginning therapists sometimes make responses to move the conversation to a shallower level because they are uncomfortable or unsure what to do when what would be more beneficial to the client is to move it to a deeper level.

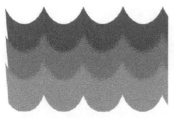

Shallower: Response reduces the depth of the conversation and lightens it.

Maintain: Response keeps the depth of the conversation the same.

Deeper: Response deepens the conversation.

Figure 3.2   Conversation Depth

I (Dr. Morris) talk in practicum class about statements and responses to our clients being on a continuum of productivity, rather than right or wrong as beginning clinical students tend to see them. Those statements, reflections and questions which move the conversation deeper are more productive and those that move the conversation in a more shallow direction are less productive toward the treatment goal.

Parrot

Parroting is the most basic form of reflective response. It is simply repeating verbatim what a client has just said. When used intentionally, it can be quite powerful, but if over-used, it can be annoying and redundant. If the therapist repeats words or phrases without active listening, it can also convey that she is only half-listening, that she heard the words but was not truly paying attention. Imagine the childhood game of mimicking everything a person says and that provides a good example of how not to use parroting. As you are active listening, watch for clues that the client is irritated or thinking, "I just said that." Those are cues that you are over-using parroting. However, if you are actively listening, it is more likely that you will perceive that you are over-using it before the client.

Purposes of Parroting

By repeating a client's words exactly, you can strategically do three things: assure the client that you are listening, punctuate a phrase and point out a pattern with repetition. The first purpose is helpful with rapport-building, and the second two are helpful with meaning making. The key to effectively using a parrot reflection is to use it purposefully.

Assurance

First, parroting can provide a simple assurance that you are listening without disrupting the thread of the conversation. This is helpful with talkative clients who speak quickly without pauses, especially early in your therapeutic relationship. It is not a full interruption, but it communicates that you are staying with them as they tell their story. It may also help you prompt the client to go a little deeper or keep from straying off on a tangent.

Client:	So I told her that I didn't wear her dress, but she didn't believe me.
Therapist:	She didn't believe you.
Client:	No, she even called me a liar…

In this example, the therapist has conveyed an assurance of listening but is also learning information that may point to core needs. More on that in the next chapter, but in this short exchange, the therapist has learned that it seemed to hit a nerve when the client was not believed and called a liar, possibly pointing to a core need of inner value that can be revisited later after you have built more rapport.

The therapist's response here deepened the level of the conversation by parroting back what seemed to be causing the client distress. The therapist could have used a different parroting response to make the conversation shallower or deeper, though (see Figure 3.3).

Shallower: *You didn't wear her dress.* This is simply a fact or detail that does not reflect the client's perspective.

Maintain: *You told her you didn't wear her dress.* This response reflects the client's perspective, but does not highlight what might be problematic.

Deeper: *She didn't believe you.* This deepens the conversation because it highlights that the problem is not what happened with the dress at all, but that the client was not believed. The client's next response does go deeper. Not only was she not believed, but she was called a liar.

Figure 3.3 Conversation Depth Using Parroting

Emphasis

Second, a parrot response adds emphasis to what the client is saying. If clients use poignant words or phrases, you emphasize them by repeating them. If clients use harsh words in negative self-talk, it can be powerful to hear those words spoken from someone else in a safe environment to recognize how they speak to themselves. When repeating what a client has said, you are not saying it as truth or agreement, but merely reiterating what the client believes and expressing an understanding from the client's perspective.

Client:	When she broke up with me, I lost everything.
Therapist:	You lost everything. Everything.
Client:	Well, not everything. I still have the dog, but I lost all that mattered.
Therapist:	You lost everything that mattered.
Client:	Yeah, I thought we were going to be together forever, but now we're not.
Therapist:	You lost your dreams for the future.
Client:	The future and the present. Who am I without her?
Therapist:	You lost your identity, too.
Client:	(sighs) I just … I lost everything.
Therapist:	(sighs) You lost everything.
Client:	I had to move out, I lost our friends, and I don't know what do with myself anymore.
Therapist:	You lost it all, your home, your friends, and who you are.
Client:	What do I do now?
Therapist:	What *do* you do now? You lost everything that matters.
Client:	I start over, I guess.
Therapist:	One thing you can do is start over.
Client:	I don't want to start over.
Therapist:	Starting over is hard when you've lost so much.

In this example, the therapist parroted the word *lost* and the phrase *you lost everything* to emphasize the losses the client was grieving in addition to the loss of the relationship. Before moving forward, this client needs the space to recognize how big this loss was and the impact physically, socially, and emotionally. The therapist was also able to challenge the all-encompassing idea that the client lost every single thing by repeating the client's phrase, "You lost everything. Everything." After allowing the client to deeply feel the multiple losses, the therapist could then circle back and help the client identify things still retained by pointing out, "You've lost a lot, but something you still have is your dog."

Patterns

Another helpful use of a parroting response is to aid the client in identifying patterns of which they may be unaware. This generally works best with a parrot and then your observation. The parrot response draws attention to the word or phrase, and the repetition emphasizes it. This is helpful in uncovering core needs that are more universal than a specific situation.

Client:	I'm so afraid that I might see him again around town.
Therapist:	You're afraid you might see him again.
Client:	Yes, and if that happened, I couldn't handle it.
Therapist:	You couldn't handle it if you saw him again. That's interesting because earlier you used that same phrase – I can't handle it – when you were talking about that conversation with your boss, another male who seems to be more powerful than you.
Client:	Yeah, but my boss didn't assault me. He's actually a nice guy.
Therapist:	The situations are different, but in both you tell yourself, "I can't handle it."
Client:	I guess I do. I hadn't thought of it like that before.
Therapist:	What does "I can't handle it," mean to you?
Client:	That I'm weak. I'm not in control of the situation, and other people make the decisions and determine what happens.

This example uncovers a similar response to two different kinds of people that is hinted at by the client's phrase, "I can't handle it." Though one is a "nice guy" and one assaulted her, the underlying perception of the client is that the other person has power and control and the client is weak. Focusing the therapeutic work on that deeper core need provides healing in both situations, though only one brought the client to seek help.

Paraphrase

Paraphrasing is similar to a parrot response in that you reflect back very similar content to what the client told or showed you, but with the distinct difference that you rephrase the response into your words instead of saying it exactly as the client did. This means that you can increase awareness

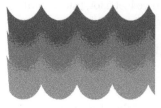

Shallower: *It made you want to rip off his head.* This highlights something outside the client: It made you…

Maintain: *You wanted to rip off his head you were so irritated.* This response reflects the client's perspective, but does not link any new information.

Deeper: *You wanted him to feel as frustrated as you felt.* This response is a risk because it is not directly what the client said, but at what was hinted. It reflects what is deeper than what has been said

Figure 3.4 Conversation Depth Using Paraphrasing

by saying it differently, expand emotional identification, or build core need vocabulary. Paraphrasing is a higher-level reflective response than parroting, but it can still be highly effective in rapport building and increasing trust in the therapeutic relationship.

Awareness

Sometimes, when a client hears what is said repeated in a different way, it makes it sound different. It may prompt a clarification or a denial. Remember that it is important that you communicate that you are trying to understand, not that you are right. In clarifying to help you understand, the client also clarifies or shifts his own understanding.

Client: I was so irritated I just wanted to rip his head off [said while twisting fists in opposite directions and with a grimace].

Therapist: You wanted him to feel as frustrated as you felt.

This paraphrase reflects both the verbal and nonverbal content as well as information gathered from the previous conversation. The therapist could have paraphrased differently to maintain, deepen or lighten the conversation (see Figure 3.4).

Identifying Emotions

With children, building emotional literacy is often a treatment goal, but many adults also struggle to correctly identify emotions. In the previous example, the therapist labeled the feeling as frustration, which is a generic, but safe, emotion word. Frustration can be multiple emotions twisted together, so it sometimes helps to begin with a generic emotion to facilitate helping the client identify more specific emotions.

Client:	I was so irritated I just wanted to rip his head off [said while twisting fists in opposite directions and with a grimace].
Therapist:	You wanted him to feel as frustrated as you felt.
Client:	I was frustrated! The beast really ticked me off!
Therapist:	Part of that frustration was anger.
Client:	No, I wasn't angry. I just thought it wasn't fair that he got credit for my idea.
Therapist:	So you *weren't* angry about the injustice of it.
Client:	Okay, I was a little angry. He took my idea, and now they think that he is great, and I'm just sitting there like a gray blob.
Therapist:	You're just a little bit angry that your idea got him recognition while you were left unnoticed, like a gray blob.
Client:	No, I'm more than a little bit angry, but if I explode I'll just feed into the stereotype.
Therapist:	You feel it, but you can't show it because then you'll be noticed for something negative, and that doesn't get you the kind of recognition you really want.
Client:	Right.

This client struggled with being able to be authentic, probably suggesting the core need to be valued. Although clearly angry, the client had compelling reasons to not admit anger, so the therapist paraphrased that denial with a little exaggeration, "So you *weren't* angry about the injustice of it" and, "You're just a little bit angry." Again, using a paraphrase to identify emotions could maintain, deepen, or lighten the conversation (see Figure 3.5).

Shallower: *That would reinforce the stereotype.* The therapist may be curious to explore what the client means by stereotype, but it keeps the focus on something external to the client.

Maintain: *If you explode, it confirms what they believe.* This response reflects the client's perspective, but likely does not add any additional awareness.

Deeper: *You feel it but you can't show it because then you'll be noticed for something negative...* This moves the conversation closer to the painful conundrum of desiring to be valued, but fearing that taking credit for the idea would have the opposite result.

Figure 3.5 Conversation Depth Using Paraphrasing to Identify Emotion

Core Need Vocabulary

Like building emotional literacy, identifying core needs helps the client understand what deep seated issue is causing the pain they feel. However, be warned that paraphrasing responses that identify core needs are often zingers. They cut directly to the pain point, and they should be used with caution, and only after a trusting, safe, therapeutic working alliance has been created. To the client, these may feel like being stripped naked, and that kind of vulnerability must be handled with care by the therapist.

Therapist:	You feel it, but you can't show it because then you'll be noticed for something negative, and that doesn't get you the kind of recognition you really want.
Client:	Right.
Therapist:	You want to be praised and valued for this great idea.
Client:	It was mine, but he acts like he thought of it.
Therapist:	And if you get mad and claim it now, they'll just see you as an angry black woman, not as a brilliant member of the team.
Client:	That's the story of my life. Other people get what should be mine, and I get shut down because all they see is what is on the outside.
Therapist:	You need them to see who you really are.
Client:	That would be nice.
Therapist:	You need them to accept and value who you are on the inside, who you really are and not shut you down, discounting your anger as a stereotypical black woman.
Client:	[whispers] Yes.

You'll learn more about core needs in the next chapter. Saying them out loud can be very powerful and liberating, but it may be painful at first. For the client above, hearing another person understand what it is like to live in a world of perceived prejudice during most professional interactions must happen before working through solutions to create lasting change. The problem is not the anger, the idea stealing or even the prejudice. The problem is that this client needs to believe she has inherent worth and value. She strives for that by avoiding negative stereotypes, and the consequence is that she cannot be her authentic self. When she fears that others doubt her worth and value, she does, too. This leaves her unable to even admit that she is angry when a colleague takes credit for her work.

Paraphrase with a Hunch

The final reflective response is the most difficult. It requires being fully present in the moment with your clients, absorbing all the information they are sharing through words, expressive arts, and nonverbal communication, and filtering that through your professional knowledge. It partners intellect with intuition. Learning to do this well takes practice, and therefore time, but this skill separates mediocre helpers from the life-changers. It is essential to continue learning throughout your career to sharpen this skill.

Paraphrase with a hunch reflects information that the client has expressed explicitly and implicitly. It is analogous to interpretation, but we argue that it is the client's interpretation that we are only reflecting back to them, since it is based on the content shared by the client. These are often phrased as *I wonder* statements.

I wonder if being called a liar hurts because she doubts you.

I wonder what would happen if you said you were furious out loud.

I wonder what would be different if you were the one who was in control.

In Creative Play Therapy, combining the skills of reflective listening and reflective responses with the knowledge of how the process works and the client's core needs informs the hunches that are reflected back to the client. You may be wrong, and that is okay. You never have all of the information, and that is why they are hunches. These are usually best used during the meaning-making phase because they may prompt change, and the client is not fully ready for the change process until then. If you have a hunch at an earlier phase, mentally note it, but you will probably not say it aloud yet.

Sitting in Silence

Now that you have learned how to strategically use reflective responses to maintain, deepen, or lighten the conversation, it's equally important to know when to say nothing. In Creative Play Therapy, talking is supplemental, and there will be times when talking will prohibit the client from being able to do the needed healing work. When the client's experience is predominantly in the right brain (creative, emotional or nonverbal), then a response that encourages the client to think will pull him out of that experience and slow or stop the work that is happening. Let your body language communicate your presence and know that you do not need to be talking to be doing your job.

Exception: Client safety always comes first. If a client is dissociating, re-experiencing trauma, or otherwise being harmed, then talk to facilitate safety. Use conversation to move the client back to thinking in the left hemisphere of the brain (yes/no questions work well here) and use grounding exercises to root the client in the present time and space. This is important protection for clients and for their ability to trust you in the future to not push them further than they have the resources to handle. Silence allows the client to inwardly dig deeper. Asking closed questions brings it up to a safer, shallower level. Healing happens at the deeper level, but you never want clients to drown at depths in which they are not able to swim. We want to maintain work in the window of tolerance (Siegel, 2010).

Silence and Creation

Often, but not always, clients will slip into silence while creating their art. Some creations are more cerebral and some clients process more easily with words, so watch your client for clues. How the client approaches the work is the right way. Notice where they are looking. If they are concentrating on what they are creating, a question would be intrusive. If they are awkwardly looking away or throwing quick glances at you, the silence is uncomfortable. Notice facial expressions. You can usually tell when something is happening internally and when they are ready to start processing. Often, clients will start talking first when ready.

Silence and Emotional Expression

When a client expresses strong emotion, it is natural to want to soothe and reduce the distress. That is what a friend would do, but your role is to walk the journey through that emotion with the client. The client must feel to heal. This is the time to create a safe space for the client to experience the depth of the emotion, a luxury that may be challenging to do outside your office. While intense, it is usually short-lived. However, other than an empathic reflection – "This is hard" or "It hurts so badly" – most talk will detract. Instead, mirror the client's body language as appropriate, sigh when the client sighs, and watch for cues about when they are ready to talk again.

Silence to Slow Things Down

Sometimes, you want to be silent to slow down what is happening. Maybe you need time to catch up with the client to reflect accurately. Maybe the client needs a few more seconds to think. Maybe what they just communicated was powerful and you both need a little time to absorb it. Sometimes silence invites the client to stay with something longer instead of rushing past what might be important. Silence slows.

Rogers' Core Conditions of the Therapeutic Relationship

Carl Rogers, the father of the person-centered theory of therapy, maintained that, "If I can provide a certain type of relationship, the other person will discover within himself the capacity to use that relationship for growth, and change and personal development will occur" (Rogers, 1989, p. 33). That was his hypothesis regarding the facilitation of personal growth during a speech at Oberlin College in Ohio in 1954. He defined the characteristics for providing that certain type of relationship as empathy, genuineness and unconditional positive regard.

Skill: Sitting in Silence

Practice saying less. Keep your responses short, and develop comfort with sitting silently with clients. Give your clients quiet space to contemplate creation. Honor the depth of pain by not saying soothing phrases that may seem trite. Slow down the session with silence, making it acceptable to say the unsaid, feel what has been numbed, and express shame and vulnerability while receiving unconditional positive regard.

Genuineness

A therapist who is genuine is aware of his or her own feelings and willing to experience and express those feelings. This means not hiding behind a professional mask. Rogers wrote, "It is only by providing the genuine reality which is in me, that the other person can successfully seek for the reality in him" (Rogers, 1989, p. 33). This means that the therapist can be her real self while also creating a safe space for the client to be her real self, too. Rogers believed this was the first condition because it is so important.

We are often asked about the boundary between being completely genuine and wholly professional. Should a therapist cry in front of a client? What if the therapist is shocked by what the client says? Would the therapist tell a client that he is bored? Clearly there is a place for maintaining a professional space. Yet, in Rogers' theoretical approach to counseling and psychotherapy, he would argue that it is essential to the relationship to be real. *We suggest this question to help you determine what or how much to share:*

> 'Is your response about you or the client?'

As long as it is client-centered, it is probably appropriate to share. That means that sobbing out of your own sadness, appearing appalled by a client's choices because they disagree with your own values, or yawning out of boredom are inappropriate because they are about you. However, at times you may cry with a client as an acknowledgement beyond words of their sorrow. You may honestly say that you are surprised, and, yes, you may challenge a client by noticing that you are bored with the client's narrative and inquiring if the client has noticed that reaction from others.

We have found that this concept of genuineness is very freeing. It allows us to be fully present without the distraction of tamping down who we are as the helper in the room. It also frees us to use our most valuable tool to the fullest, the person of the counselor. Being highly effective at genuineness is predicated on two things. First, therapists must know themselves well enough to identify what they are feeling. Second, therapists need to identify whether their responses are about them or the clients. In addition, therapists need to determine those two things quickly in the moment. Like the other core conditions that Rogers identified, these are learned skills even though some are naturally better at it than others.

Unconditional Positive Regard

The next core condition is what we describe as believing that all clients have inherent worth simply because they exist. Rogers described unconditional positive regard early on as acceptance and wrote that,

> By acceptance I mean a warm regard for him as a person of unconditional self-worth – of value no matter what his condition, his behavior, or his feelings… This acceptance of each fluctuating aspect of this other person makes it for him a relationship of warmth and safety, and the safety of being liked and prized as a person seems a highly important element in a helping relationship.
>
> (Rogers, 1989, p. 34).

When the therapist truly has unconditional positive regard for the client, it frees the client to explore areas that are unsavory or shameful, whether those feelings are real or perceived. It creates a relationship where clients can share thoughts, feelings and behaviors that would risk censorship in other relationships. It is essential for a safe therapeutic working relationship.

Empathy

We believe that Rogers' final condition, empathy, is the most important of the three core conditions, but it is built on the foundation of the first two. Empathy is trying to understand the client's world from the client's perspective. There is a cartoon that shows this well. It has two characters looking at a number from opposite sides. To one, the number looks like a nine and to the other it looks like a six, even though they are looking at the same thing. Empathy is working with the client to understand how what you believe to be a nine is a six from the client's perspective, and during your therapeutic time together, it is indeed a six.

In practical terms, it might mean reflecting back what seems like an affirmation of truth when a client shares that the childhood abuse was her fault, even though you clearly know that it was not, because you understand how she came to that conclusion. You are validating her perspective, not the truth of it. (Do not worry. When you truly understand the client's perspective, you make space for change, including the client being able to say or show you that maybe it was not her fault. That shift is more powerful than you challenging her conclusion before you understand how she came to believe it.)

Rogers wrote,

> It is only as I *understand* the feelings and thoughts which seem so horrible to you, or so weak, or so sentimental, or so bizarre – it is only as I see them as you see them, and accept them and you, that you feel really free to explore all the hidden nooks and frightening crannies of your inner and often buried experience .
>
> (Rogers, 1989, p. 34).

Summary

Much of the work that begins to shift into change in Creative Play Therapy happens in the creation and expressive stages, which are often much less

verbal or even nonverbal phases. This is why we maintain that talking is supplemental. To facilitate the work in those stages, therapists must become
adept at active listening, reflective responses, and sitting in silence. These
skills need practice to sharpen them, but they greatly enhance the therapeutic
working relationship and improve outcomes. After all, is that not what we
want, to be highly skilled and highly effective in our work?

References

Cozolino, L. (2017). *The neuroscience of psychotherapy: Healing the social brain* (3rd ed.). New
York, NY: W. W. Norton & Co.
Green, E. J., Drewes, A. A., & Kominski, J. M. (2013). Use of mandalas in Jungian play
therapy with adolescents diagnosed with ADHD. *International Journal of Play Therapy,
22*(3), 159–172. doi:10.1037/a003371910.1037/a0033719 supp (Supplemental).
Landreth, G. L. (2012). *Play therapy: The art of the relationship* (3rd ed). New York: Routledge.
Peabody, M. A., & Schaefer, C. E. (2016). Towards semantic clarity in play therapy.
International Journal of Play Therapy, 25(4), 197–202. doi:10.1037/pla0000025
Perryman, K. L., Moss, R., & Cochran, K. (2015). Child-centered expressive arts and play
therapy: School groups for at-risk adolescent girls. *International Journal of Play Therapy,
24*(4), 205–220. doi:10.1037/a0039764
Rogers, C. R. (1989). *On becoming a person.* Boston, MA: Houghton Mifflin.
Siegel, D. J. (2010). *The mindful therapist: A clinician's guide to mindsight and neural integra-
tion.* New York, NY: W W Norton & Co.
Van der Kolk, B. A. (2014). *The body keeps the score: Brain, mind, and body in the healing of
trauma.* New York, NY: Viking.
Wheeler, N., & Dillman Taylor, D. (2016). Integrating interpersonal neurobiology with
play therapy. *International Journal of Play Therapy, 25*(1), 24–34. doi:10.1037/pla0000018

What Are Core Needs?　**4**

The thing that makes Creative Play Therapy different from other therapeutic approaches is the use of expressive arts to do deep work on core needs. To be able to do that, however, you need to know what core needs are and how to identify them. Now that you have the tools from the last chapter to respond in reflective ways that help the client move deeper, this chapter will help you see and hear which core needs are being expressed.

At times symptom relief is the most important work that needs to be done. When a client is suicidal, feeling extreme distress from symptoms, or in crisis, deep therapeutic work is not possible, or preferable, until the client is stabilized. At these times, the therapist needs to focus on decreasing the distressing symptoms.

Most times, however, therapists spend too much time on symptoms. There are good reasons for this. First, the symptoms are probably the presenting concerns that clients came to you to resolve. Second, symptoms are easier to measure for treatment outcomes. Finally, it seems easier to tackle, say, panic attacks than what may be underlying them. Yet, if you want your client to experience healing, those deeper contributing factors are exactly where the therapeutic work needs to be done.

The problem with only working on symptoms is that, without addressing the root of the problem, it comes back. Using the panic attack example, maybe the client does experience relief from panic attacks for a few months, but gradually they increase in frequency again. Or, perhaps you do a great job educating the client on how to manage them and they reduce substantially in frequency and duration, but the client begins having migraine headaches.

The symptom comes back in a different form. Symptoms can be psychosomatic, mental chatter, or emotional in nature, but whatever form they take, they are the body's way of communicating a problem, so they are helpful at pointing to the core need that is not being met, but if those symptoms are ignored, then they either increase in severity or change forms.

Identifying Core Needs

Working with client issues is like weeding dandelions. Those white, fluffy balls of seeds serve a purpose for the plant. If you want to remove the weed from the yard, however, those seeds cause more problems. Picking the flowers will not get the weed out of the yard. You must get the root, but dandelion roots are hard to address without careful deep work (see Figure 4.1). Doing nothing just creates more symptoms by letting it go to seed, so if you want to remove the weed, then you must remove the root cause. Creative Play Therapy helps therapists to facilitate the deeper level root work on core needs.

Figure 4.1 Core Needs and Symptoms

How do you identify a client's core needs? Theorists in the social sciences have categorized them in different ways. Maslow outlined five levels of needs, Beck identified basic needs stemming from cognitive beliefs and Glasser offered five genetic needs. While other conceptualizations of core needs exist, this book will build on these to present a simple model for identifying core needs in Creative Play Therapy.

Maslow's Hierarchy of Needs

One of the best-known conceptualizations of needs for motivating action stems from Abraham Maslow's Hierarchy of Needs (Maslow, 1943). See Figure 4.2. He began with basic needs that are universal to all people, the physiological needs and once a person's needs are satisfied (or generally satisfied) at that level, then that person is motivated to satisfy safety needs, then social needs, esteem needs and finally the need to self-actualize. Maslow's important contribution was not to identify the needs that most people have, but to classify those needs in levels of importance, a hierarchy. When lower-level needs are not met, higher-level needs are less important or not relevant at all.

A category of need that many clients have unmet is the need for safety, especially clients who have experienced trauma. With adults, the physical

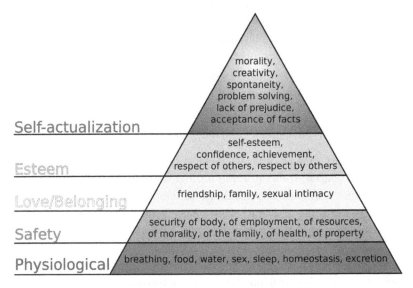

Figure 4.2 Maslow's Hierarchy of Needs

safety concerns may seem to be met, yet *emotional* safety needs remain. For example, a client may have experienced childhood abuse in another state from a person who has died, yet remains highly vigilant in relationships and has difficulty even trusting the therapist. Maslow addressed this when he wrote (Maslow 1943, p. 395):

> Any thwarting or possibility of thwarting of these basic human goals, or danger to the defenses which protect them, or to the conditions upon which they rest, is considered to be a psychological threat. With a few exceptions, all psychopathology may be partially traced to such threats.

Beck's Core Beliefs

Aaron T. Beck, the founder of cognitive theory, believed that people develop ideas about themselves, others and the world beginning in childhood. Those core beliefs become absolute truths that are so fundamental and deep that they are not even recognized by the person (Beck, 2011). His daughter, Judith Beck, identified three core cognitive beliefs: lovability, adequacy and helplessness – as examples, the client believes "I am undesirable," "I am incompetent" or "I am trapped" – (Wenzel, 2012) that often underlie the problem. When the therapist listens for cognitive distortions in those areas, the therapeutic work is greater than addressing situational cognitive distortions. While this categorization is probably too simplistic for all clients at all times, it provides an excellent framework for filtering the information from the client. In session, it is easy to remember three broad categories and learn phrases and patterns that indicate one of the core cognitive beliefs.

Glasser's Five Needs

William Glasser, creator of reality therapy, believed that all people have five genetic needs: survival (self-preservation), love and belonging, power (inner control), freedom (independence and choice) and fun (enjoyment) (Glasser, 1999). The first two are quite similar to Maslow's needs, but identifying a genetic need for power, freedom and even fun, was quite different. Glasser believed that all long-lasting problems were relationship problems. For clients who have experienced being overpowered by a parent, another person, society or systems, the need for power and control (not the need *to* control) can be very important, and it is one of the core needs we will include in the core needs pyramid.

The Core Needs Pyramid

Using what we learn from our professional predecessors, we have created the Core Needs Pyramid to provide an easy-to-remember framework for identifying core needs. Like in Maslow's hierarchy, some core needs are more fundamental and should be addressed first. These form the base of the pyramid. Like Beck's three core cognitive beliefs, this simple model will not fully capture the complexity of human responses to pain, but it does provide a practitioner-friendly model that is easy to remember without consulting a model. And, like Glasser, we believe these are genetic needs.

When these needs are threatened in childhood, the impact can last a lifetime and generally are more enduring. A client who fears being able to take care of basic needs for the first time as 35-year-old adult will likely be more adept at managing the risk than a similar adult client who also has childhood history of scarcity around food and housing. Childhood crises may make these clients more vulnerable.

The Core Needs Pyramid is intended to be a model for working with clients in pain. It does not address higher-level needs such as fun or self-actualization, although we believe those are important, too. Instead, it hones in on the basic needs that many of our clients have experienced being unmet, and working with a client to meet these needs can be life-changing and healing. The basic core needs are the need for safety and security, power and voice, inner value and relationship (see Figure 4.3).

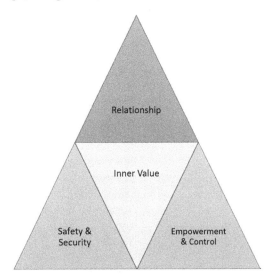

Figure 4.3   Core Needs Pyramid

Safety and Security

Starting at the base of the pyramid, the two most basic core needs are for safety and security and for empowerment and control. If at any time the client has perceived these needs to be unmet, then they are likely to resurface again, even if the need is met currently. For example, if a child experienced food scarcity, then even as an adult with a surplus of food in the pantry, she may still feel debilitating anxiety when the meteorologist predicts a winter storm and suggests stocking up on food and water or she may begin hoarding food to an excessive degree, both symptoms of her core need for safety and security.

Consider things that might threaten a person's safety or security for a moment. Anything that ever risked food, shelter, clothing and transportation would be in this category. Anything that could be harmful would also be in this category, including harm from self or others, natural disasters, or life-threatening medical diagnoses. Separation from family, not being safe around those who should be safe and feeling abandoned also fit in this category. In uncovering this core need, listen for themes around the following topics (see Table 4.1).

Empowerment and Control

The next core need is about being empowered and having the ability to voice your needs without dangerous consequences. The symptom might be to dominate or be controlling, but the core need is to be autonomous and

Table 4.1   Safety and Security Core Need Themes

Safety and Security Core Need Themes	
Needs	**Fears and Symptoms**
Survival	Abandonment
Basic Needs	Separation
Physical Safety	Disease/Medical Concerns
Emotional Safety	Harm
Financial Security	Hunger
Protection	Neglect
Nurturing	Death

Table 4.2   Empowerment and Control Core Need Themes

Empowerment and Control Core Need Themes

Needs	Fears and Symptoms
Power	Perfectionism
A Voice	Disordered Eating
Being Heard	Rescue Fantasy
Strength	Anxiety
Justice	Hopelessness
Fairness	Helplessness
Spiritual Will	Chaos
Spiritual Protection	Instability
	Aggressiveness
	Rigidity
	Inflexible
	Controlling

directive of one's own life. Any experience of being overpowered by another (physically, mentally or emotionally) is likely to activate creative play themes in this area, including not having a voice, desiring justice and perfectionism (see Table 4.2). Spiritual issues may appear in any of the core need categories, but in our experience, they most often manifest here in the challenge of understanding an all-powerful deity who has allowed bad things to happen and the clash between wills. We'll say more about this in Chapter 14.

Inner Value

The next core need is the inherent need for worth and value (Table 4.3). This includes themes relating to love, mattering to others and being able to care for oneself. In the Core Needs Pyramid, this need is nestled inside the others and these core needs are about who we really are down deep, so they may not be readily apparent *early in treatment or without thorough assessment.* Any attempts to mask or be inauthentic are an indication of inner value core needs.

Relationship

Some core needs are evident within the context of social relationships. Remember to always consider the three other core needs as well because

Table 4.3   Inner Value Core Need Themes

Inner Value Core Need Themes

Needs	Fears and Symptoms
Worth	Compensations
Value	Perfectionism
Lovability	Workaholic
No Prejudice	Overly Dependable
To Matter	Must Appear Competent
Self-Sufficiency	Wearing a Mask
Resilience	Too Independent
Integration	Controlling
Healthy Independence	Afraid to Ask for Help
	Codependent
	Not Mattering
	Not Being Enough
	Enduring Suffering or Mistreatment

Table 4.4   Relationship Core Need Themes

Relationship Core Need Themes

Needs	Fears and Symptoms
Trust	Abandonment
Intimacy	Grief
Attachment	Loss
Committed Love	Isolation
Honest Friendship	Loneliness
Autonomy	Shame
Reparation	Dependency

relationship needs may also be an indication of unmet safety and security, empowerment and control and/or inner value core needs. However, these individual needs that we have seen in our work are also influenced by living and working in a Western culture. In cultures that are more collectivist, there may not be an unmet individual need if it is not perceived by the client. Also, we are relational beings and having relationships with others is a need. See Table 4.4.

It is important to realize that these needs develop from the client's perception of the situation, and they may or may not be real threats to the needs. For example, a child might hear his parents fighting about his misbehavior at school, and when they tell him they are getting a divorce, his perception is that he caused the divorce because of his bad behavior and is therefore bad. As you work with this client many years later as an adult, he may have the cognitive knowledge that the marriage dissolved after an affair, not a phone call from the school, but because he experienced the perception that *he* ruined his parents' marriage, he may struggle with the core need for inner value.

It is also important to note that the client's perception of the situation determines which core need is threatened. In the previous example, the same child might have instead perceived his mother as incapable of taking care of him risking his security or his dad's leaving as the trigger of a series of negative events that risked his safety. Or, the core need that he perceived not being met could have been power and control, since other people made decisions for him that he did not want, such as the judge who awarded custody to the parent he did not want to see. Key to understanding core needs is an empathic understanding of the client's world.

Often, there is more than one core need that emerges. In these cases, listen to understand which one seems to be a greater need for the client. When in doubt, start with the needs at the base of the pyramid and work your way up. With relationship core needs, be particularly attuned to possible deeper level core needs as well. A need for power could look like a relationship core need, but the underlying need might be an individual need to have inner control, not really about being controlling in an intimate relationship.

Summary

Understanding the four basic core needs allows us to group themes and understand what is rooted in the soil beneath those dandelion symptoms. Symptoms themselves do not identify which core need is unmet. The client's perception does. A client's inability to leave her house may suggest a safety need, but if she cannot leave her home because she fears that she will cause bad things to happen to those around her if she does, it is more likely an inner value need. These lists, then, are guidelines, not rules.

Creative Application: Assemble a Starter Creative Kit

Begin to practice Creative Play Therapy by assembling a small starter creative kit. Try it out with a client or, if you are still a student, practice in a skills class or on yourself. If you already like one of the expressive arts discussed in Chapter 2, gather a few supplies for using it.

If you are not sure where to start then we would suggest starting with some basic art and writing supplies: blank paper, writing instruments and colored pens/pencils. Add some three-dimensional figures: people and animal figures, soldiers, landscape materials, spiritual items, a bridge, fences, vehicles, fidget toys, etc. which could later be used with photography or sand tray.

For now, keep your starter creative kit simple. Allow yourself time to explore what you truly like using with clients and to what your clients seem to respond. As you grow in experience and comfort with the expressive arts, your preferences might change, so starting with the basics reduces the expense and any expectations you might inadvertently set for yourself and your clients.

References

Beck, J. S. (2011). *Cognitive behavior therapy: Basics and beyond* (2nd ed.). New York, NY: Guilford Press.

Glasser, W. (1999). *Choice theory: A new psychology of personal freedom*. New York, NY: HarperPerennial.

Maslow, A. H. (1943). A theory of human motivation. *Psychological Review, 50*(4), 370–396. doi:10.1037/h0054346 Retrieved from: https://doi.org/10.1037/h0054346. Accessed February 17, 2020.

Wenzel, A. (2012). Modification of core beliefs in cognitive therapy, standard and innovative strategies in cognitive behavior therapy. In I. R. D. Oliveira (Ed.), *Modification of core beliefs in cognitive therapy, standard and innovative strategies in cognitive behavior therapy*, Retrieved from www.intechopen.com/books/standard-and-innovative-strategies-in-cognitive-behavior-therapy/modification-of-core-beliefs-in-cognitive-therapy.

How Does Understanding 5
Development Grow
Empathy?

It makes sense that we need to understand development when working with children, but what about adults? We know that children grow quickly and experience significant cognitive, physical and interpersonal changes, but why do we need to conceptualize adults through developmental models? With the explosion of developmental theories, which ones help us to holistically understand our clients?

Why Developmental Models Are Helpful

It is important to understand human development for three reasons. First, since we often work with adults with issues that happened or began in childhood, it is helpful to understand where the client was developmentally at the time. Sometimes, it helps us understand why the client copes in certain ways, and what needs are being expressed. The term *developmental trauma* was coined to formally recognize that early trauma is different (Olson-Morrison, 2017). Knowing this increases our ability to better understand the world from the client's perspective.

Second, development continues into adulthood. Even though many developmental models lump adulthood into one category, an 18-year-old is developmentally at a different place than a 40- or 65-year-old. Viewing adult clients through a developmental model increases our understanding of where they are now.

Third, the strength of stage models of development is to gain a general understanding of what is normal development and what is not in a variety of areas. Although not a perfect description for every individual, stage models help with an overview of the entire person: physical, social, cognitive, moral, spiritual and identity development. In Creative Play Therapy, we strive for overall healing, not segmented pieces of healing, so knowledge about how people develop optimally and how clients have experienced disruptions in development is important.

Despite the variability in completing developmental tasks, there are consistencies that help us understand how our clients adapt across the lifespan. McCormick et al. (2010) list seven tenets of developmental task theory (p. 124):

1. Developmental tasks emerge and change as a function of development in context.
2. Some developmental tasks are universal.
3. Some developmental tasks are culturally or contextually specific.
4. Developmental tasks include multiple dimensions or domains of behavior.
5. Success and failure in age-salient developmental tasks forecasts success and failure in later developmental tasks.
6. Success or failure in developmental tasks often has cascading consequences.
7. Strategic intervention focused on developmental tasks can promote success and positive cascades while preventing problems and negative cascades.

Limitations of Developmental Models

While developmental models are very helpful, Ray (2011) offers three cautions about misunderstanding them. First, the stages and descriptions of the models may overlook the uniqueness of the child. She writes, "There should be restraint on the part of the play therapist to generalize to every child, in every context. The uniqueness of the child and child's environment is the play therapist's first concern" (p. 18). This applies to adults as well, since adults are unique and the therapist empathizes with the client's world from the client's perspective. Second, Ray cautions that developmental models offer a conceptualization of average, so those who do not fit those descriptions may be viewed as deviant or pathological. People develop at their own pace, and though they may need additional therapeutic help at times, it does not always indicate abnormality. Finally, Ray cautions about what she calls the "Race to the Top" (p. 19), the idea that higher levels of development are better. Achieving higher levels or stages does not translate to better functioning, sense of belonging or positive emotional state. In fact, being advanced in one area of development can be problematic.

As you progress through the following stage model discussion, keep in mind that these are models of average development. The clients you see may be (or may have been) operating at a higher or lower level of development because of their experiences and understanding of those experiences. For the purposes of Creative Play Therapy, it is less important to identify whether the client is above or below the average than to understand what each stage of development indicates about how clients make sense of their situations and develop beliefs from their understanding, which influences how they act, feel and think.

Five Areas of Development

We have noticed a trend in the field of developmental psychology towards very specific areas of development. We are going to try to do the opposite. Our aim is to provide an overview of five areas of development – physical, social, cognitive, moral and spiritual development – and then pull them together in a concise model to use as an aid to communicate empathy, or understanding of the world from the client's perspective. Then, we will additionally provide an overview of identity development, which often does not follow chronological age development. The result will at times be an oversimplification of an entire field of study, but the purpose is to provide a helpful, practical framework for you to consider past and present development of your adolescent and adult clients. Most programs in the helping professions require a course on development, so this should be a brief overview and synthesis of a few of the traditional models. As with any learning, our aim is for you to fully understand the basics and then add to that knowledge in ways that are more specific to your experience and understanding. This chapter is not intended to be comprehensive.

Below, we will provide a narrative overview of five stage models of development. Then, we will put them together side by side in tables for quick reference. You are probably most familiar with tables from your development classes, but what we want to do here is use the tables to pull all the areas of development together by age. If you like tables, then you can flip ahead for reference in the next section.

Physical Development

The first category provides the guide for the remaining areas of development, since most of these theorists created categories based on chronological age. While a medical model of physical development is beyond the scope of this book, if you are working with a client who experienced significant advances or delays in physical development, be aware of the impact of those. For example, an 8-year-old who begins menstruating while in in a third-grade classroom taught by a male teacher may feel the impact in several developmental areas in addition to physical symptoms. Ask the client about the impact when in doubt. "What was it like to be the first girl in your class to start your period?"

Richard Havighurst first coined the term *developmental tasks* and the concept that new tasks arise as people move into new stages (Horton-Parker & Brown, 2002). They are sequential and build on previous stages, so disruptions at one stage may be problematic at later stages as well. He divided the lifespan into six categories and included physical, social, cognitive, moral and existential tasks together, which is why we have included it first, as an overview. He and his co-authors wrote, "These are the common major tasks – certain learnings, adjustments, achievements – that face all individuals in a given society or sub-group of society; they are the modes of cultural adjustment expected of an individual and rewarded by his society" (Schoeppe et al., 1953).

In Early Childhood, approximately birth to age six, Haivghurst believed that children first learn tasks around eating solid foods and controlling elimination. They also gain skills for walking, talking and learning gender differences. Children begin to form a conscience and distinguish right from wrong, and they acquire language skills and form concepts.

In Middle Childhood, ages six to 12, they navigate how to get along with peers. They become more independent and develop skills in reading, writing and math. They learn concepts for living. Older children begin to understand gender-appropriate social roles, acquire democratic attitudes and develop a personal set of values.

Adolescence is the years between 12 and 18. The tasks during this time include achieving more mature peer relationships, preparing for a career and gaining increased independence from parents. Adolescents continue in their development of personal values and an ethical ideology. In this stage, they also have the task to achieve socially responsible behavior.

Early Adulthood extends from about age 18 to age 30. During this stage of development, young adults form intimate relationships and learn to live with a partner. Family tasks in this stage include starting a family, raising children and managing a household. This stage also includes getting started in a career and achieving civic responsibility. Socially, this stage means finding a congenial social group.

Just as a reminder, stage theories do not mean that all people do these tasks, by choice or by circumstance. It means that they experience the challenge of each task and negotiate what it means for them if they do not "achieve" it. For example, if a client dates little and marries at age 40, she will have resolved the early adulthood tasks of forming an intimate relationship and living with a partner, but because she has not done it during that stage, she experiences the implications as she participates in friends' weddings, shops for other people's baby gifts, experiences loneliness, advances in her career and travels extensively. She has to negotiate the intimate and social tasks whether she intentionally chooses to wait to marry, cannot find an interested partner, or selects a socially unconventional option.

Ages 30 to 60 in Havighurst's model is Middle Adulthood. This stage includes the generations before and behind, so in it, adults help adolescent children become independent and care for the older generation. Relationships with partners change as the focus becomes less on co-parenting. Coping with illness and deaths of parents, family and friends is another task. The tasks also include trying to maintain satisfactory careers, assume civic leadership roles and develop appropriate leisure activities, while adjusting to physical changes from aging.

Late Adulthood extends from age 60 to death. The tasks in this stage include adjusting to decreased strength and chronic health problems, retirement and satisfactory living arrangements. They deal with the death of a partner and staying connected socially. They also must face mortality and accepting their life (Horton-Parker & Brown, 2002).

Psychosocial Development

Erik Erikson expanded Havighurst's concept of the early childhood years and conceptualized each stage as the resolution of a challenge. He simplified the tasks to just ones that related to psychosocial (physical and relational) challenges. The strength of his model is the recognition that the resolution might be positive or negative, and how a stage is resolved impacts future stages.

Erikson (Horton-Parker & Brown, 2002) divided what Havighurst called early childhood into three separate stages. He called the first stage Infancy, birth to 18 months, and he identified the challenge as trust vs. mistrust. The task in this stage is for babies to develop adequate trust in the world (*and people*) and assume that it is a safe place. In Early Childhood, from ages one to three, toddlers develop control over their actions and gain a sense of being a separate person. The challenge is autonomy vs. shame and doubt. Preschool, ages three to six, involves acquiring a willingness to try new behaviors and assuming responsibility for personal actions, and the challenge is initiative vs. guilt.

Erikson's School Age, ages six to 12, corresponds with Havighurst's Middle Childhood stage of development. The challenge is industry vs. inferiority. During this stage, children must resolve developing confidence in their abilities and the ability to get along with peers. Adolescence, ages 12 to 18, also fits in the same timeline as Havighurst's model. Erikson identified this challenge as identity vs. role confusion, and the task is to achieve a strong sense of self by trying out many possible identities.

For adulthood, Erikson and Havighurst divide the stages similarly, but Erikson did not specify ages. In Young Adulthood, the task is to form a lasting and committed intimate relationship, and the challenge is intimacy vs. isolation. For Middle Adulthood, the task is to assist the younger generation in getting started in the world, and the challenge is generativity vs. stagnation. Finally, in Maturity the task is to accept your life as meaningful and satisfactory, and the challenge is integrity vs. despair.

Cognitive Development

To navigate developmental tasks requires thinking and using cognitive processes to gain an understanding of the world and how to live in it (Horton-Parker & Brown, 2002). Jean Piaget described developmental tasks through the lens of cognitions. His model outlined four stages.

The Sensorimotor stage (Horton-Parker & Brown, 2002), birth to two years, covers the same period of development as Erikson's Infancy stage. Cognitively, infants experience life in the here and now. They use reflexes and simple motor skills to explore the world as they look and grasp. All cognitions are in early development. While they navigate Erikson's challenges of trust and independence, that learning is based mostly on visual and tactile information.

From ages two to six, young children are in the Preoperational stage. They use symbols and language to represent the world. They are able to form simple concepts, but their understanding is egocentric. They have difficulty with logical operations such as classification, conservation and seriation. This is why children in this stage want what appears to be the biggest cookie, call all petaled plants flowers, believe that a wider container holds more, and may use the words yesterday and tomorrow incorrectly. Children are developing foundational vocabulary to begin to be able to verbally describe objects. Combining this with Erikson's Preschool stage, children are trying new things, including how they use symbols and language. Because they are naturally egocentric, but developing responsibility for personal actions, they can attribute responsibility to themselves when they are not responsible. This tension between initiative to try new things and guilt for what happens has lifelong implications when trauma occurs during this stage.

Ages seven to 11 is the Concrete Operations stage. During this time, children can think logically about concrete objects and events. They understand logical operations, but cannot yet grasp hypothetical concepts. Children at this age can begin to verbally describe their inner experiences, but they may have difficulty conceptualizing alternate scenarios. When doing therapeutic work with children in this stage, you may see evidence that cognitions exceed the capacity to express them verbally, which may falsely indicate that they are not capable of the cognitions. As we weave this with Havighurst's Middle Childhood and Erikson's School Age stages, the two main tasks are to develop confidence in their abilities and get along with peers. While navigating peer hierarchies, these children struggle with understanding alternate scenarios. They may internalize other-given labels because they understand logically why they were identified that way, but may not understand alternate explanations yet.

Formal Operations is Piaget's last stage of cognitive development, and it extends from age 12 and beyond. In this stage, adolescents and adults think logically about abstract and hypothetical concepts. They have the capacity to consider what could be, rather than only what is. This covers four stages from Havighurst and Erikson. During these four stages, adolescents are resolving the challenge of identity, and adults are working through issues of intimate relationships, legacy and a meaningful life. Clearly, these require the cognitive capacity to consider abstract and hypothetical concepts about love, family, personal influence, lasting impact, disease and death. And this very cognitive ability can make these issues very complex.

Moral Development

Lawrence Kohlberg, who was influenced by Piaget's study of children's moral development, created a matrix model to show the results of his 20-year longitudinal research (Horton-Parker & Brown, 2002). His theory has critics, but he established moral development as a distinct field with a distinct theory, methods and domain, as well as moving away from Piaget's biological focus to an emphasis on social theories (Vozzola, 2014). His model included three stages with two levels in each stage, confusingly referred to as numerical stages, so in the descriptions below, remember that the numbered stages are within the three identified stages. Progression to the next level requires increasing cognitive complexity. Besides specifying morality in cognitive development, Kohlberg's model introduced a half-step stage of development. This recognized that while a person might still be within a certain stage, early developmental levels and advanced developmental levels within that stage are different.

Since moral development is a cognitive process, Kohlberg's first stage did not begin until age five, when a person is cognitively capable of representative symbols and language and can form simple concepts. At this point, the person has resolved (positively or negatively) the Eriksonian challenges of trust and autonomy and is in the process of resolving initiative. They have skills, according to Haivghurst's model, for walking, talking, learning gender differences, forming a conscience and distinguishing right from wrong.

The Pre-conventional stage of moral development begins with Stage 1, ages five to seven, and this task is understanding punishment and obedience. In this child's mind, bad things are punished and good things are rewarded. Those in authority have power to mete out the punishments and rewards. It happens during Piaget's Concrete Operations stage, when children think logically and concretely. Stage 2, from eight to 12 years, is when behavior is judged by hedonistic outcomes, or how it affects me. These pragmatic children expect that if they do something for someone else, that person should do something for them. This is Erikson's School Age stage, when getting along with peers and developing confidence in abilities is the task. Kohlberg's explanation provides the moral rules for negotiating authority and peer relationships.

The Conventional stage of development starts at age 13, and people may or may not progress to the next stage. This stage corresponds with the Adolescent stages described above, and moral judgments are based on conforming to others' expectations, maintaining social approval and complying with external authority mandates (Horton-Parker & Brown, 2002). In Stage 3, ages 13 to 16, acts are considered moral if they garner social approval, what Kohlberg called the good boy-nice girl orientation (Kohlberg & Wasserman, 1980). In Stage 4, age 16 and older, acts are judged based on adherence to rules, laws and external authority. This moral reasoning happens while adolescents are trying out many different identities and developing their personal values. They are considering career options and becoming more independent from their parents. If an adult remains in this stage, then right and wrong continue to be determined from external sources.

Kohlberg's final stage of moral development is the Post-conventional stage, and it occurs in adulthood, if at all. At this stage, morality is evaluated based on individual rights (an internal orientation of right and wrong) so it moves past personal rewards and social expectations of the previous stages. In Stage 5, morality is based on honoring social contracts, and it allows for a relativist view of personal values (Horton-Parker & Brown, 2002). In other words, we do not have to believe the same things, but we follow social conventions to cooperate and coexist together. In Stage 6, morality is a combination of personal ethics and universal consideration of everyone, things such as equality, justice and dignity for all people.

As you become more familiar with the stages, it provides more information to increase empathy. If, for example, you work with an adult client who lost his mother at age eight, you quickly understand that he was coping with something for which he was not yet developmentally ready. That event "normally" happens in middle adulthood, during the Post-conventional stage, but he experienced it at school age, during the Pre-conventional stage, without the growth and development in between. While it is likely a significant loss at either stage, the eight-year-old could be especially concerned about how it impacts him, and the unfairness of it, while the adult may readily accept a need to grieve, but also be concerned about the impact on his own children. When painful events happen out of order, it likely has an isolating effect, too, because it feels aberrant.

Spiritual Development

James Fowler used the term faith to broadly describe a trust and loyalty to a transcendent center of value and power, not a specific faith belief or religion (Horton-Parker & Brown, 2002). Fowler believed that the capacity for faith development was universal and cross-cultural. His model was hierarchical, but, like Kohlberg, he did not believe that all people reached the higher stages. Although some critics argue that some of his conclusions still lack empirical support (Parker, 2010), it is still a valuable model to consider.

In Chapter 14, we will delve more into spirituality. When people experience emotional pain, it impacts their faith, whether they define that as a religion or another system of beliefs, what Fowler refers to as *ultimate reality*. Pain brings up difficult existential questions, and when our clients live in it, their belief systems will likely change, possibly creating ripple effects in their families and communities. Therefore, understanding how these spiritual beliefs are developed is important to understanding the entire person. It also cues you about whether these beliefs are an area of strength or an area of challenge for your client. Regardless, it allows you to ethically, from a client-centered perspective, work on spiritual issues in therapy.

Fowler began with the Pre-stage: Undifferentiated Faith, which occurs in infancy. This stage is when seeds of trust, hope and courage compete with fears of abandonment. How tasks relating to physical, psychosocial and cognitive development are resolved will influence whether these seeds are hopeful, trusting and courageous or fearful, and thus will impact all future stages (Horton-Parker & Brown, 2002).

Stage 1: Intuitive-Projective Faith happens in early childhood. This stage is when self-awareness emerges. According to Fowler's model, intuition guides the child's understanding of their relationship to an ultimate reality, and their imagination fills in gaps in understanding (Horton-Parker & Brown, 2002). Imagination at this stage is unrestrained by logic (Erwin, 2001). Therefore, children who are still developing the verbal ability to express cognitions understand faith intuitively. When there is limited knowledge, cultural taboos or misconceptions, the child may develop terrifying fantasies. They project that faith concretely through scary fantasies when they do not understand. The moral task at this stage is understanding punishment and obedience and an egocentric understanding of what they get from social exchanges.

Stage 2: Mythic-Literal Faith occurs in middle childhood. In this stage, reality is literal, symbols are one-dimensional, and rules are considered real and concrete (Horton-Parker & Brown, 2002). They construct cause-and-effect perspectives to understand the world, which are incorporated into stories and myths (Erwin, 2001). In middle childhood, children are navigating peers, going to school and learning social roles. Children in this stage may not yet fully grasp hypothetical concepts.

Stage 3: Synthetic-Conventional Faith occurs in adolescence. Adolescents attempt to understand social relationships while determining morality through social approval and later based on rules and external authorities. In this stage of faith development, they also use the qualities they have experienced in personal relationships to understand the value and power of an ultimate reality.

The next stage occurs in young adulthood. Stage 4: Individuative-Reflective Faith is when self-identity and personal worldviews start to become differentiated from others, and young adults form their own interpretations of ultimate reality (Horton-Parker & Brown, 2002). This stage is marked by critical reflection as an awareness of the complexity of life arises. This may be a time of disillusionment with previous beliefs. As young adults are valuing intimate relationships and merging families, beliefs that were comfortably unquestioned before may now be examined through a new perspective. Higher education, friendships not influenced by parents and career values may also create the friction that adds to differentiation. This may not be a despairing disillusionment, though. They are in Piaget's Formal Operations stage, and have the capacity to consider things that could be. Many young adults enjoy this new freedom and exposure to new ideas. Others find that their previous beliefs are solidified, but as personal, not external, beliefs.

In mid-life, Fowler describes the Conjunctive stage as a time of integrating unrecognized issues from the past, a time when the past is reclaimed and reworked to create new meaning. During this stage, heightened spiritual revelations are possible. This is when adults are heavily invested in the generation before and behind and coping with illness and deaths in friends and families. A seriousness arises as they seek to cultivate an identity and meaning for others (Erwin, 2001). They are trying to meet Erikson's challenge of generativity vs. stagnation. Moral development, if they have developed past the need for social approval, is usually with an internal sense of right or wrong that is less concerned with what they get in return.

Stage 6: Universalizing Faith is the final stage of faith development. This stage is rarely achieved, but when it is, it is marked by extreme compassion and may involve martyrdom for faith. Those that reach this stage are often more appreciated after death. It corresponds with Kohlberg's Stage 6, where a concern for universal ethics for all people occurs.

Synthesizing the Five Chronological Areas of Development

Now that you have an overview of five of the areas of development, let us put them together side by side to get a snapshot of how clients typically view the world at various ages by seeing the developmental tasks grouped together. A full understanding of these tasks will inform your active listening and how you reflect the information the client is giving you. The stage names and chronology are cited from *The Unfolding Life: Counseling Across the Lifespan* (Horton-Parker & Brown, 2002). The following tables summarize the developmental theories side by side and chronologically for your quick comparison.

Identity Development

There are many models of specific identity development that are helpful in grasping how people proceed with understanding who they are, and we encourage you to learn from them. Like the previous stage models of development, each stage in identity development builds on the previous one, but unlike the previous models, these are not associated with chronological age. Like all stage models, progress is presented in a linear fashion, but higher levels are not better, just more developed. This is an entire field of study itself, so this section will be an over-simplification of identity development that focuses on process only, not the content of the development. We strongly encourage further reading in this area.

Similar patterns exist, regardless of the identity that is being developed that can be conceptualized through stage models. It may be ego identity, personal identity or social identity (McLean & Syed, 2015).

Table 5.1   Infancy Stage

Approximately Birth to 2 Years				
Havighurst Tasks Development	*Erikson Tasks Psychosocial*	*Piaget Tasks Cognitive*	*Kohlberg Tasks Moral*	*Fowler Tasks Faith*
Early Childhood	**Trust vs. Mistrust**	**Sensorimotor**		**Pre-stage:**
Eating solid foods	Developing adequate trust in the world to assume that it is a safe place	Infants experience life in the here-and-now, and use reflexes and simple motor skills, such as looking and grasping, to explore the world		Undifferentiated faith
Controlling elimination				Foundation for later faith development
Walking	**Autonomy vs. Shame and Doubt**			
Talking				Seeds of trust, hope and courage compete with fears of abandonment
	Developing control over one's actions and a sense of being a separate person			

Table 5.2 Early Childhood Stage

		Approximately 2 to 5 Years (Preschool)		
Havighurst Tasks Development	Erikson Tasks Psychosocial	Piaget Tasks Cognitive	Kohlberg Tasks Moral	Fowler Tasks Faith
Early Childhood	**Autonomy vs. Shame and Doubt**	**Preoperational**	**Pre-conventional:**	**Pre-stage:**
Learning sex differences	Developing control over one's actions and a sense of being an independent person	Young children use symbols and language to represent things in their world and are able to form simple concepts.	Stage 1: Punishment and Obedience orientation	Undifferentiated faith
Forming a conscience				Foundation for later faith development
Distinguishing right and wrong	**Initiative vs. Guilt**	Their understanding is egocentric and animistic, and they have		Seeds of trust, hope and courage compete with fears of abandonment
Acquiring language	Acquiring a willingness to try new behaviors and to assume responsibility for one's own actions	difficulty with logical operations such as classification, seriation and conservation		
Forming concepts				

Table 5.3 Middle Childhood Stage

	Approximately 6 to 12 Years (Elementary School)				
Havighurst Tasks	*Erikson Tasks*	*Piaget Tasks*	*Kohlberg Tasks*	*Fowler Tasks*	
Middle Childhood	**Industry vs. Inferiority**	**Concrete Operations**	**Pre-conventional:**	**Stage 2:**	
Learning to get along with peers	Developing confidence in one's own abilities, the ability to get along with peers and developing a sense of self in relation to others.	Children are able to think logically about concrete objects and events, and can understand logical operations. They cannot yet grasp hypothetical concepts.	Stage 1: Punishment and Obedience orientation	Mythic-Literal Faith	
Becoming more independent			**Conventional**	Reality is interpreted literally	
Developing skills in reading, writing and math			Stage 2: Instrumental Relativist orientation	Symbols are one-dimensional	
Learning needed concepts for living				Rules are considered to be real and concrete	
Understanding gender-appropriate social roles				Ultimate reality is understood through anthropomorphic characters in cosmic stories	
Acquiring democratic attitudes					
Developing a personal set of values					

Table 5.4 Adolescence Stage

	Approximately 12 to 18 Years				
Havighurst Tasks	Erikson Tasks	Piaget Tasks	Kohlberg Tasks	Fowler Tasks	
Adolescence	**Identity vs. Role Confusion**	**Formal Operations**	**Conventional:**	**Stage 3:**	
Achieving more mature peer relationships	Achieving a strong sense of self by trying out many possible identities	Adolescents can think logically about abstract and hypothetical concepts and can consider possibilities of what could be, rather than just what is.	Stage 3: Interpersonal Concordance or Good Boy-Nice Girl orientation	Synthetic-Conventional Faith	
Preparing for a career				Ultimate reality is structured in	
Gaining increased independence from parents			Stage 4: Law and Order orientation	interpersonal terms with images of unifying value and power derived from	
Continuing to develop personal values and an ethical ideology				qualities experienced in personal relationships	
Achieving socially responsible behavior					

Table 5.5 Young Adult Stage

			Approximately 18 to 30 Years		
Havighurst Tasks	*Erikson Tasks*	*Piaget Tasks*	*Kohlberg Tasks*	*Fowler Tasks*	
Early Adulthood	**Intimacy vs. Isolation**	**Formal Operations**	**Post Conventional (Possibly)**	**Stage 4:**	
Forming intimate relationship	Developing the ability to form a lasting and committed intimate relationship	Adults can think logically about abstract and hypothetical concepts and can consider possibilities of what could be, rather than just what is.	Stage 5: Social Contracts and Relativist Personal Values	**Individuative-Reflective Faith**	
Learning to live with a partner				Self-identity and worldview become more differentiated from others	
Starting a family					
Raising children				Own interpretations of ultimate reality are formed	
Managing a household					
Getting started in a career				Critical reflection and awareness of complexity of life arises	
Finding a congenial social group					
Achieving a civic responsibility				Disillusionment with previous beliefs may occur	

Table 5.6 Middle Adult Stage

	Approximately 30 to 60 Years				
Havighurst Tasks	Erikson Tasks	Piaget Tasks	Kohlberg Tasks	Fowler Tasks	
Middle Adulthood	**Generativity vs. Stagnation**	**Formal Operations**	**Post Conventional (Possibly)**	**Stage 4 (Possibly)**	
Helping adolescent children become independent	Assisting the younger generation in getting started in the world	Adults can think logically about abstract and hypothetical concepts and can consider possibilities of what could be, rather than just what is.	Stage 5: Social Contracts and Relativist Personal Values	Conjunctive Faith	
Learning to again relate to one's partner as a person, rather than a parent			Stage 6: Universal Ethical Principled orientation	Unrecognized issues from past become integrated into self	
Caring for the older generation				Past is reclaimed and reworked to arrive new meaning and deeper awareness	
Coping with illness and deaths of parents, family and friends				Heightened spiritual revelations are possible	
Maintaining satisfactory career				**Stage 5 (Rarely)**	
Assuming civic leadership roles				**Universalizing Faith**	
Developing appropriate leisure activities				Extreme clarity and compassion	
Adjusting to physical changes associated with aging				May involve martyrdom for faith and being more appreciated after death	

Table 5.7 Older Adult Stage

	Approximately 65 Years and Beyond				
Havighurst Tasks	*Erikson Tasks*	*Piaget Tasks*	*Kohlberg Tasks*	*Fowler Tasks*	
Later Adulthood	**Integrity vs. Despair**	**Formal Operations**	**Post Conventional (Possibly)**	**Stage 4 (Possibly)**	
Adjusting to decreased physical strength and chronic health problems	Accepting one's life as having been meaningful and satisfactory	Adults can think logically about abstract and hypothetical concepts and can consider possibilities of what could be, rather than just what is.	Stage 5: Social Contracts and Relativist Personal Values	Conjunctive Faith	
Achieving satisfactory physical living arrangements			Stage 6: Universal Ethical Principled orientation	Unrecognized issues from past become integrated into self	
Adjusting to retirement				Past is reclaimed and reworked to arrive new meaning and deeper awareness	
Dealing with the death of a partner				Heightened spiritual revelations are possible	
Staying connected and maintaining social relationships				**Stage 5 (Rarely)**	
				Universalizing Faith	
Facing mortality and accepting one's life				Extreme clarity and compassion	
				May involve martyrdom for faith and being more appreciated after death	

We offer a simplified version of identity development that can be informative with a variety of difficult labels: child of divorce, alcoholic, rape survivor, epileptic, infertile, parent who lost a child, single again, natural disaster survivor, cancer (or other medical diagnosis) patient, abused, failure, etc. Hammack (2015) described it this way (p. 11), "Identity is the anchoring concept for thinking about difference and sameness in our time." However the client identifies as the same or different is identity. The client may phrase these descriptors differently, but often work is around accepting an unwanted label, such as victim, addict or depressed. Keep in mind that anger described below may not be traditional anger, and clients may express these stages in a variety of ways. Below you will find how we conceptualize identity development stages.

Stage 1: Unawareness

At this stage, people are unaware of or unaffected by the identity or labels. They may not even know this identity exists. If they do, it is so removed from them that they do not know (or know they know) anyone directly with the identity.

Stage 2: Denial

Awareness is dawning and the person suspects or knows that the identity might be true, but it is a secret. Subtle or overt attempts to deny or mask the identity occur.

Stage 3: Revealing

This stage includes an internal, but not yet external, resignation to the identity. The person knows that this is their identity, but is reluctant to publicly admit it. At some point, however, what has previously been hidden is now revealed. It could be by choice to a few trusted individuals. Or, it may not by choice, for example through a court decree, arrest, scandal, or being found out.

Stage 4: Anger and Declaration

This stage is often marked by growing anger and perhaps an at times off-putting declaration of the identity. After living with and possibly fighting the secret identity, the person now may need to vocalize it, join groups around the identity, and begin to advocate. They may want to educate themselves and seek help with the identity.

Stage 5: Identity Internalized

At this point people firmly understand that the identity is part of who they are, but it does not define them. They have an acceptance of the identity, and they can be accepting of those who are in other stages regarding identity development, including unawareness.

While this model may not perfectly fit every client, it will help you conceptualize how to work with your clients, boosting your unconditional positive regard. Working on acceptance of the identity is not something that a client in Stage 2 is ready to do. Insensitive opinions may be expressed by the client when in Stage 1. Understanding that you may not see anger as an emotion until stages 3 or 4 will help you trust that your client knows what is needed.

General Identity Development

Stage 1: Unawareness

Stage 2: Denial

Stage 3: Revealing

Stage 4: Anger and Declaration

Stage 5: Identity Internalized

Putting All Areas of Development Together

Our thesis throughout this chapter is that understanding your client increases empathy and unconditional positive regard. In this chapter, we have attempted to explain how to understand client development – physical, social, cognitive, moral and spiritual – by looking at slices of time with the five types of development for the client, rather than looking at isolated types of development (i.e. cognitive) across a life. By having this holistic understanding, the therapist can hone in on the present, and at chronological points where a disruption occurred.

What we have referred to as identity development – which could be anything from being Southern to being gay … or both – is not linked with physical age. It happens in linear process, too, though. Figure 5.1 shows the five types of development across slices of time with the identity process of development happening underneath it all.

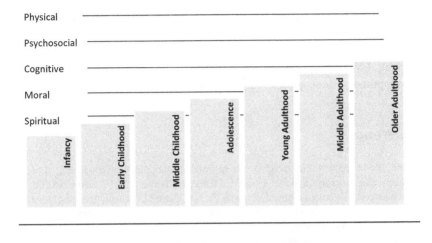

Figure 5.1 Development Map

Creative Application: Timeline

Create a timeline of five significant events in your own life. Now identify in what stage of development those events took place. Plot the events on the development map above. Consider your developmental tasks. How do they relate to your identified core issues?

Summary

Development can be conceptualized through stage models for physical, social, cognitive, moral and spiritual development. The life stages are Infancy, Early Childhood, Middle Childhood, Adolescence, Young Adult, Middle Adult and Older Adult, and each stage has specific tasks. This provides a framework for understanding when your client faced challenges in the past, what challenges they may be facing currently, and which challenges are inherent or out of step in development. Layering identity development helps you facilitate acceptance of an unwanted or undesired label. As you understand development, you also increase your understanding of the rationale behind why a client tries to meet unmet core needs in unhelpful ways based on their development. Most importantly, when you understand child, adolescent and adult development, you gain higher levels of empathy for the client.

References

Erwin, T. M. (2001). Encouraging the spiritual development of counseling students and supervisees using fowler's stages of faith development. In P. Hammack. (2015), *Theoretical foundations of identity*, New York, NY: Oxford University Press, pp. 11–31.

Hammack, P. L. (2015). *The Oxford Handbook of Identity Development*. (McLean, K. C., & Syed, M. U., Eds.). Oxford University Press, pp. 11–30.

Horton-Parker, R. J., & Brown, N. W. (2002). *The unfolding life: Counseling across the lifespan*. Westport, CT: Bergin & Garvey.

Kohlberg, L., & Wasserman, E. R. (1980). The cognitive developmental approach and the practicing counselor: An opportunity for counselors to rethink their roles. *The Personnel and Guidance Journal, 58*(9), 602–605.

McCormick, C. M., Kuo, S. I.-C., & Masten, A. S. (2010). Developmental tasks across the lifespan. In K. L. Fingerman, C. A. Berg, J. Smith, & T. C. Antonucci (Eds.), *Handbook of life-span development*, New York: Springer Publishing Company, pp. 117–140.

McLean, K. C., & Syed, M. U. (2015). The field of identity development needs an identity: An introduction to *the Oxford handbook of identity development*. In K. C. McLean, & M. U. Syed (Eds.), *The Oxford handbook of identity development*, New York, NY: Oxford University Press, pp. 1–10.

Olson-Morrison, D. (2017). Integrative play therapy with adults with complex trauma: A developmentally-informed approach. *International Journal of Play Therapy, 26*(3), 172–183. doi:10.1037/pla0000036.

Parker, S. (2010). Research in Fowler's faith development theory: A review article. *Review of Religious Research, 51*(3), 233. Retrieved from https://search.ebscohost.com/login.aspx?direct=true&AuthType=sso&db=edsjsr&AN=edsjsr.20697343&site=eds-live&scope=site&custid=s8863735

Ray, D. C. (2011). *Advanced play therapy: Essential conditions, knowledge and skills for child practice*. New York: Routledge.

Schoeppe, A., Haggard, E. A., & Havighurst, R. J. (1953). Some factors affecting sixteen-year-olds' success in five developmental tasks. *The Journal of Abnormal and Social Psychology, 48*(1), 42–52. doi:10.1037/h0054913.

Vozzola, E. C. (2014). *Moral development: Theory and applications*. New York, NY: Routledge.

Part II

Stages of Creative Play Therapy

Creative Play Therapy is distinct from traditional talk therapy, so the process looks different. Yet, while there is tremendous variability from individual to individual, the stages of the process are remarkably predictable. While the chapters in this section will describe the overall therapeutic process, you will also likely see clients progress through these stages quickly, sometimes in just one session. When that happens, it usually resolves the specific issue, but the client may cycle through the stages multiple times before resolving a Core Need. For example, in one session, a client may work on a triggering event that happened recently, and after the session, his or her response to that situation changes, but more work still needs to be done on the Core Need that led to the symptom that caused distress.

Because this process can move very quickly, it is essential to understand the importance and purpose of each stage so that the therapist knows when to slow things down. Check in with clients when in doubt. They are the experts on themselves, and sometimes you will not know without asking.

Although based on the nondirective client-centered approach, when working with adults, prompts can be helpful to facilitate the nondirective work. We will talk about when, if and how to prompt in each phase. We'll also suggest a sample creative technique that is appropriate for each phase.

The Creative Play Therapy approach has seven phases which are displayed in Figure 0.2.

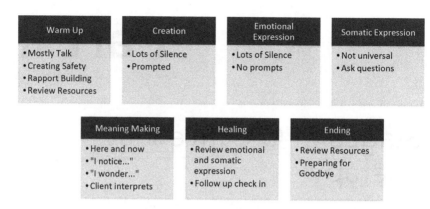

Figure 0.2 Overview of Stages of Creative Play Therapy

Warm Up   6

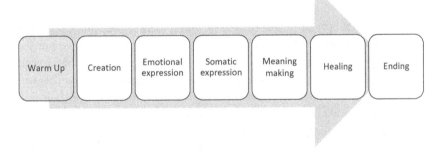

Figure 6.1 Stages of Creative Play Therapy

Now that we have laid the groundwork for Creative Play Therapy – establishing our theoretical lens, developmental understanding and some basic skills – we are ready to expand on the stages of the process. The very first stage of any counseling relationship is the warm-up stage. Before you can do meaningful work together, you need to get to know each other and build a trusting professional relationship. Clients who have been hurt may naturally be cautious about trusting others, or they may have poor boundaries and trust too easily, and move through this stage too quickly. At any point if you experience any damage to the therapeutic working relationship, come back to this stage. The Warm Up lays the foundation for and weaves through every other stage.

The first few minutes of every session should also start with a warm up. It helps your client ease into the work with you. If you have been working together for a while, then the client probably has experience with the deep work of this approach, but they need a few minutes to warm up to get themselves ready.

Warm Up develops the healthy, safe relationship needed to do the deep work on core issues. This is not something you check off so you can get to doing therapeutic work. This is the work. During this phase, you are modeling healthy relationship skills, including repairing the relationship when needed. If you spend an entire six sessions warming up with a client, that may be the very work that is needed for that client. If a client is not truly able to do deep work, even when he says that he would like to do it, then he will not be able to do it. It may not be a safe time for him yet, and it may not have anything to do with the therapist. More about this in Chapter 13. Of course, all of this assumes that the therapist is skilled and prepared to facilitate the process, and that the therapist is genuinely trustworthy.

Purpose of the Warm-Up Phase

In addition to simply getting to know each other, the warm-up phase has three purposes: to create safety, to build trust, and to assess the client (resources, history, symptoms, etc.). When you first meet a client, you are probably both nervous. Neither one of you knows exactly what to expect or how this will go. The client is often in a state where things are bad enough to seek help and may have already exhausted other options first.

Seeking counseling services is difficult for some. Clients feel weak and vulnerable, and based on first impressions, it may seem like you have nothing in common. You may be different genders, different races, different religions. For clients, it may appear that you have it all together, while they feel like everything is falling apart. Perhaps they come from families with unspoken rules about allowing other people to see their messy problems. What could happen if they trust those problems with a stranger? Without successfully working through Warm Up, clients might not come back.

The best predictor of successful outcomes, according to Mancillas (2006), is the client's experience of feeling empathically understood. Mancillas also reported that outcomes were based on four things: client variables, such as motivation and level of pathology (40%), the therapeutic relationship which included empathy, warmth and unconditional positive regard (30%), expecting change and/or placebo effect (15%) and only a small portion for counselor techniques (15%). This means that, excluding client factors, establishing a strong working relationship accounted for about half of the positive outcomes, and the client's perception of that relationship was the best pre-dictor. Gottlieb (2019) wrote that the most important factor in successful therapy is the feeling of being felt, which matters more than the therapist's training, the treatment modality, or the presenting problem. Therefore, the time spent in the warm-up phase is well spent for laying the foundation upon which future work happens. It is also valuable to, at times, pause and spend time strengthening the relationship.

To create the strong therapeutic relationship, the first session should begin at a very shallow and safe level. This starts with the informed consent to create boundaries and establish trust, but before diving into the information from the intake forms, get to know the person (or people) in front of you. If you are new at this, it might be helpful to have a few general questions that you ask to help break the ice. We like to have the clients talking within the first 30 seconds to establish a therapeutic culture that is focused on the client. The first few questions are just about getting started, not jumping into any big topics. By adeptly beginning the session, you are establishing that you understand timing and the client's natural nervousness. This is important in creating safety. Take a minute or two to engage in small talk.

General Questions to Begin a Session

How was it finding the office?

What was traffic like today?

Did you get caught in the rain (or other weather-related question)?

Would you like some coffee or tea (if you serve beverages)?

After a little general small talk, move the conversation to a general question about the client. "Tell me a little about you," is a common one that works well. But first, observe the client. What might the client's body language be telling you? If you notice that she seems very nervous, you could normalize that with, "I am always nervous the first time I meet a client. How are you feeling?" If the client seems reserved and withdrawn, stay at a shallow level until the client is more comfortable. Remember, this is the work. In an effort to remain genuine, it could be helpful to overtly say what you are doing. "You seem pretty nervous about this. Why don't we just get to know each for a bit? How about if I ask you a few questions about things you like and things you don't? What is your favorite ethnic food?" For the first session only, it might

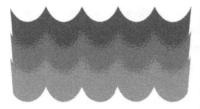

Shallow: Warm up starts here as you get to know each other and determine how you will work together. Begin at a very shallow, very safe level.

Maintain: As the client begins communicating about more real content, you will move to this level. Most of the warm-up phase will be here or shallower.

Figure 6.2 Depth of Warm Up

be helpful to provide a loose framework for what you have planned, while still keeping it client-centered, to help clients know what to expect.

Part of the skill set needed for Creative Play Therapy is knowing when to facilitate shallow work and when to facilitate deep work, knowing how to guide the process with intention. Once there is a comfortable dialogue between you, then intentionally move toward the other purposes of the warm-up stage. This will take some time, but remember that building the relationship and safety is the work, not a prelude to the work, so the time spent in this warm-up stage is well invested. Now, let's talk about the goals of the warm-up stage.

Skill: Rapport Building

Rapport building is a skill, and it can be learned. Some people have natural aptitude for beginning relationships, and they tend to do a few things comfortably. First, they maintain appropriate eye contact. Second, they lean toward the person in an expression of interest. Third, they often nod and say short words or phrases to convey that they are listening. Fourth, they do not have physical barriers between themselves and the other person, such as a desk, table, notepad, clipboard or laptop. Fifth, they are aware of the other person's body language and adjust the previous four things to make them more comfortable. For example, if the client is leaning back in his chair, the therapist will also lean back, giving the client more space. Finally, they understand silence and allow extra time when the other person is thinking or having trouble formulating words, but ease awkward silences when the client is waiting. Good rapport happens when the other person feels heard and as if you are trying to understand (not necessarily that you understand perfectly).

Create Safety

Even as you engage in small talk for the first couple of minutes, you want to intentionally create physical and emotional safety for the client. Many people have not experienced a relationship with another person where they show their biggest vulnerabilities or areas of shame and still receive acceptance, so even if they hope for that with you, they may not believe that it will really happen.

UNCONDITIONAL POSITIVE REGARD

We discussed this in more depth in Chapter 3, but it is the best way to create emotional safety. Facilitating all of the core conditions helps create a safe space for your client, but unconditional positive regard warrants special mention. Clients will often test you with small revelations and gauge your response to see if they can trust you with more. If they think that you are unable to hold their pain, they will not trust you with it. If they think you will judge them for their choices, they will not trust you with them. And, if they think you are faking a response (not being genuine), they will not trust you. Cultivate safety with unconditional positive regard, valuing the client regardless of their thoughts, feelings or actions. "I hear your shame about that, but it seems to me that you were trying to protect yourself in the best way you knew how at the time."

KEEP BOUNDARIES

Boundaries are essential for safety. Fences keep pets and children safe. Highway barriers keep drivers safe. Limits in sessions keep clients safe. Time management around ending sessions is challenging for many practitioners, but having the skills and awareness to end a session on time lets clients know that you value their time, too, when they are the one waiting or they have other obligations after your session. You may need to set a boundary preventing a client from going deeper than they are ready to go or when you do not have enough time to fully process it. Finally, you may need to establish boundaries to ground a client in the here and now, pausing the work when it gets too overwhelming. Be transparent with clients as you do this. "I notice that your breathing has gotten shallow and you look scared. Let's pause right there to make sure you are okay. What's happening with you right now?"

PREPARE THE CLIENT TO LEAVE

While you may think of safety during the session, to facilitate client trust in you and the process, you also want to create safety after and between sessions. Therefore, how the sessions end and what the client does between sessions is also important for the client's safety and willingness to engage in this work with you. When clients experience a deep or difficult session, make sure you allow a few minutes at the end of session to prepare them to walk out of the office. Deliberately bring the session up to a shallower level. If clients have been crying, allow them time to take a few deep breaths and prepare themselves in whatever ways they need. Ask clients what happens next and what they need. For example, some clients might want to sit alone in the car for a few minutes. What will it be like walking to the car? Who will be seen on the way? Once in the car, what will be helpful? What happens after that? What will it be like to eat dinner tonight? How do they anticipate sleeping tonight will go? What kinds of self-care activities work well and how can those be incorporated? If you are doing trauma work, this is also a good time to talk about how to structure the scheduling of sessions so the client can take care of themselves afterward (such as take a nap, be alone, or be with supportive friends). You want the client to take steps to provide extra care for themselves during Creative Play Therapy.

Build Trust

Creating safety relies on counselor skills, but trust relies on client factors. While there are things you can do to help build trust, ultimately, it will be up to the client to trust you. Until the client trusts you, it is not safe to move into deep work, so stay at a comfortable level of depth until the client is ready. If a client has difficulty trusting, that likely has more to do with their experiences than you. Model trust by trusting your clients to know when they are ready. Below are a few things you can to do to help build trust.

BE TRUSTWORTHY

You can tell the client that they can trust you, but the client will believe what they experience more. Therefore, it is important that you provide evidence of your trustworthiness. Be direct when explaining confidentiality and the limits to that confidentiality during informed consent, but also along the way as you work together. Your honesty about when you will break confidentiality actually builds trustworthiness because it is truthful and conveys that you care about the client's safety. If the client is struggling to trust you, reflect his concerns back to him, and you might add a response to meet his need. The more you are able to accurately reflect, the more trustworthy you become.

"You're wondering if you can really trust me enough to talk about that. That seems wise since you've been hurt by people you thought you could trust. I can wait until you are ready."

PRACTICAL PROBLEM SOLVING

At times, the client may need some practical help to reduce distressing symptoms. While the bulk of this work will be on the underlying core issues that are manifesting the symptoms, the client needs to know that you understand that the symptoms are problematic, too. If, after confrontations with the boss, your client has a panic attack in the bathroom, spending time on psychoeducation for calming techniques (and learning from the client what is helpful) means that your expertise can be trusted.

Assess History, Symptoms and Resources

The final purpose in building rapport is to assess the client's history, symptoms and resources. This can be done in a comfortable conversation as you get to know the client. Listen for areas of strength and areas that are especially challenging.

"I'm going to ask a few questions about various areas of your life to help me get to know you better. You can tell me as much or as little as you like. What do you like to do in your free time?"

When assessing areas, be attuned to the things that are going well, areas of strength for the client. You will help the client draw on these when needed later. Also notice when the client is cautious about answering or when body language and words are mismatched. These probably indicate areas of vulnerability, and they may be your first clues about core issues. However, in the warm-up phase, do not press for answers. You have already learned information that cues you to revisit it later.

"That may be hard to answer right now. That's okay. Let me ask you about something else." You do not usually want to shy away from difficult content, but in the warm-up phase, you do. This response lets your client know that you understand, but also that you can ease discomfort. The warm-up phase is often awkward for clients, so having empathy, saying it out loud and addressing the need to be more comfortable will build rapport.

Below are some suggestions for areas to informally assess, but your setting will likely also have formal assessments that happen around intake, and that will shape the way you conduct assessments, diagnose and conduct clinical interviews. This chapter will not cover the cross discipline and multiple settings where that happens, who conducts them, or how extensive they may be, but we acknowledge that it is part of the therapy for the clinician. As you assess, pay particular attention to answers about physical health, as that is often the body's way of pointing to something significant. These are listed from safest to what could potentially be more uncomfortable, but they can be ordered in what way makes sense with the current client.

Important Areas to Assess

Work – type, environment, enjoyment, professional relationships

Education – current level, aspirations, regrets

Physical – overall health, eating habits, exercise, sleeping habits, medications

Current Family – current living situation, intimate relationships, significant past relationships

Friends – quantity and close friendships, friendship history, teasing, bullying, marginalization, loss

Family of Origin – nuclear family, growing up, current relationships with

Finances – comfort, distress, conflict

Hobbies and Fun – free time activities, how they play, ease of playing and recreation

---

Using Prompts in the Warm-Up Phase

Up until this point, we reviewed basic counseling skills within the context of a verbal exchange. Since adult clients often have an expectation that therapy means talking about problems, begin where the client is comfortable. This works well with traditional intake and assessment protocols, too. We almost always begin by talking, but when we think the client might be open to more creative approaches, we briefly suggest one and observe the client's reaction. If the client needs more explanation or structure, we provide it, while erring on the side of keeping it as open to the client's interpretation as possible.

Prompts are short suggestions to direct the client's creative work. If prompts are directive, how do they fit with a client-centered approach? While child-centered play therapy rarely, if ever, uses prompts, adults have been socialized to follow rules. While we like to keep the prompts as open-ended as the client is comfortable with, prompts are helpful to get things started and limit the scope of the work for that session. Because most adult clients are comfortable and expect to talk, prompts are used to introduce creative approaches, but in the warm-up phase, this is in tandem with traditional talk therapy.

Sometimes, a creative technique can help with the warm-up phase. You can use any of the expressive arts, but keep in mind the purpose of the technique. In the warm-up phase, expressive arts are used to create safety, build trust and assess the client. This is not the time (yet) for deep core need work.

If this is the first time you are introducing a creative technique, set it up for the client. More on that in the next chapter. If the client wants to adapt the technique that you suggest, that is fine, often even better. The point is not the technique or even the content in the warm-up phase, but facilitating trust, rapport and assessing the client. The following are some sample prompts.

Sample Prompts for the Warm-Up Phase

"Now that I know a little something about you, I'd like to get to know you better. I have some drawing materials here. Would you be willing to draw me your current family however you define that? Stick figures are fine, since there is not a right or wrong way to do this."

"I have some scenic photographs in this pile. Look through them and select one that makes you feel safe, and tell me about it."

"I'd like to do something a little different. How do you feel about that?.. [Assuming the client is interested ...] Okay, I'd like you to think about five significant events in your life so far, good or bad. Pick five (or more if you like) figures to represent them, and arrange them on the table in whatever way makes sense to you."

"Write a bunch of adjectives that describe you, and make the words bigger or smaller depending on how much they describe you. You can even make the words decorative if you'd like."

"You mentioned that you like listening to music. I have an idea to help me better understand how you perceive your family members. How does that sound to you? [Assuming the client is interested...] I have these instruments, and you can use anything else you think of, too. Make a sound for each person in your family and then describe why that sound fits that family member."

When and When Not to Suggest a Creative Technique

In Warm Up, prompted expressive techniques are helpful to increase client safety, comfort and trust. Most people like more structure until they feel comfortable in a new setting, and prompts can help with that. Remember that using an expressive technique in the warm-up phase has a different purpose than using an expressive technique in the creative phase. In the creative phase, you are facilitating depth, but in the warm-up phase, you are facilitating trust. This should enhance comfort and rapport, so follow the client's lead.

Below are times when it would be beneficial to suggest a creative technique.

- When a client seems very curious about the creative supplies in your office
- When a client shares an interest in the arts, alternative mediums of communication, or other creative pursuits
- When a client appears very open and highly motivated to do therapeutic work
- When your professional intuition suggests that this might helpful
- When you are not sure how a client would respond, but you would like to test it to determine how to proceed in your work together.

However, not all clients will embrace this approach, and some will need longer to warm up before being comfortable with what may feel like a vulnerable exercise. If this is the case, proceed with a traditional talk therapy approach. Perhaps later it will be appropriate to introduce a creative technique, but only if the client is amenable.

These are times when it would be best to avoid creative techniques, and if you have prompted one, scrap it and do something different:

- When a client seems especially cautious or wary
- When a client is overly concerned with revealing too much
- When a client expresses that it is stupid or weird
- When a client feels like every expression is being scrutinized for hidden meaning (it may help to explain that you do not interpret)
- When a client is highly uncomfortable.

Some clients may come to you because other people want them to get help. They have agreed to satisfy those others, but they are not yet ready to do the deep work. Honor that because the client is probably right. Pushing deep work when the client is not yet ready can be damaging. (If there are safety issues requiring dangerous behaviors to be addressed, then use an evidence-based directive treatment modality until the client is ready to do the deep work.) Some clients have experiences of others learning vulnerabilities about them and then manipulating them, and this treatment modality could seem risky and frightening. Stop the creative technique and process the client's response in the here and now with plenty of reflective responses instead. When the client feels safe, then proceed. This can really enhance rapport because you are creating an environment where the client is empowered to stop the process when it is uncomfortable and you are demonstrating that you are listening to the client and respecting the client's needs and desires.

If you are attuned to the client's verbal and nonverbal communication, then that will cue you about whether the client is ready, not yet ready, or needing a different approach. When in doubt, ask the client, especially as you are learning to understand what is being communicated without words. "I can't quite tell what you are thinking about this drawing technique. What is going through your head right now?" or "You seem unsure about picking out figures to represent your family. What's going on with you right now?" Sometimes, what seems to be resistance to the technique is simply clients trying to meet your expectations, but not knowing how, or not yet understanding that they truly have freedom in how they proceed with the prompt. This is especially common in the warm-up phase.

Any time you notice that the client is having trouble using a creative approach or moving forward in the work, pause the technique and process in the here and now. Try a reflection/question. Reflect what you observe and then ask the client to help you understand what they are experiencing. Ask follow up questions until you both understand, then ask the client what they would like to do: go back to the technique, change it, or do something different. Adolescent and adult clients can easily pause and then go back to it, and often with additional insight.

Creative Technique to Try

Instead of a specifically prompted exercise, make supplies available and invite clients to doodle, draw or write on paper while you get to know each other. Notice when it changes significantly and what is being discussed then, but do not draw attention to it yet. This is a light approach to introduce expressive techniques and enhance trust and rapport-building.

The warm-up phase is important as you establish the therapeutic relationship with your clients. It is the point in the therapy where you are intentional about creating safety, building trust and assessing the client. This is also the phase where you test out using creative techniques to learn how to best incorporate them with each individual client. Be cautious about moving to the next phase too quickly because every other phase of therapy builds on this one.

References

Gottlieb, L. (2019). Why therapists break up with their patients. *Time(April)*. Retrieved from http://time.com/5544180/why-therapists-break-up-with-their-patients/
Mancillas, A. (2006). Counseling students' perceptions of counseling effectiveness. In G. R. Walz, J. C. Bleuer, & R. K. Yep (Eds.), *Vistas: Compelling perspectives on counseling 2006*, (pp. 191–194). Alexandria, VA: American Counseling Association.

Creation

7

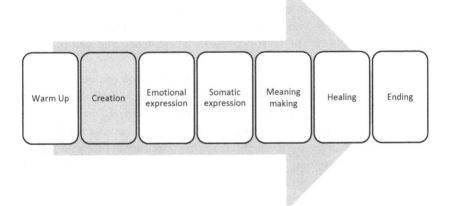

Figure 7.1 Stages of Creative Play Therapy

The creation phase is where the deeper level work really begins. On a micro level, we cycle through most of the stages in nearly every session after the strong therapeutic working relationship is built. On a macro level, the bulk or intensity of the work will be moving through the process much slower. What that means is that after the initial warm up of the relationship, which could take a few sessions, the next several sessions may focus on learning how you and your client work together creatively.

This stage allows clients to use symbols to substitute for concrete reality from a safe distance, and then share and manipulate that world of their own making symbolically (Etzi, 2004). You may try a few different expressive arts to see which seem to be easier for your client to use to communicate. Early on, you will spend more time on the creation, and the client may or may not do much emotional or physical expression, meaning making or healing yet. The stages are generally sequential, but clients may cycle through them many times before the ending of their therapeutic work with you.

The Creation Phase

In the creation phase, you will prompt your client to create some version of an expressive art that shows you what they are trying to communicate. Although Carl Rogers originated the term *nondirective therapy*, and Creative Play Therapy is grounded in his client-centered approach, nondirective helpers use directive skills at times, such as psychoeducation or training sessions, selecting supplies, and choosing which responses to reflect back (Kenney-Noziska et al., 2012). The creation stage is a time when you will be more directive.

Clients will create a product, something tangible and concrete that you can both explore together in the next phases. Often, you will use a phrase that the client has said for your prompt. It can be helpful to think *show me*.

For example, let's say that a client has come to you because she has just filed for divorce. In the warm-up phase, she has talked about how she and her husband fight all the time, her concerns about her daughter's high levels of anxiety, and her fears about making ends meet on her limited income. She has also mentioned a recent diagnosis of irritable bowel syndrome, feeling isolated from her friends, guilt that impacts her faith, and being a child of divorce herself. In the creation phase, you begin to uncover the core issues that link several of these things together.

Counselor:	How have things been this week?
Client:	Alright, I guess.
Counselor:	You guess.
Client:	Yeah. I met with the lawyer again, and we're officially filing for divorce this week.
Counselor:	You knew it was coming, but this is the legal process that makes it really happen.

Client:	What am I doing? I'm going to ruin my daughter's life. I mean, I know she'll be okay eventually, but it's going to be so hard on her. Her life will never be the same.
Counselor:	And neither will yours.
Client:	No, I guess not, but she's so young.
Counselor:	You are really worried about how this could harm her.
Client:	It's like I can't win. If I stay in this marriage, she gets hurts by our escalating fights, and I worry that he'll strike out at her, too, but if I divorce him, she's hurt by that, too.
Counselor:	You can't win, and all of you lose.
Client:	That's me, a loser.
Counselor:	And your daughter. Even your husband.
Client:	Soon to be ex-husband.
Counselor:	How old were you when your parents divorced?
Client:	Ten.
Counselor:	And how old is your daughter now?
Client:	Nine. Almost the same age.
Counselor:	I think it would help me understand what is happening with you better if you could show me what it is like. Earlier, you said that you were going to ruin your daughter's life. That was a pretty powerful statement.
Client:	I think that is what is happening. I'm ruining her life.
Counselor:	You are ruining her life. Would you be willing to show me that? What is it like for YOU to ruin your daughter's life.
Client:	What do you mean?
Counselor:	I have these miniatures on the shelves there. You are welcome to use any of those or anything else you want in this room. This box of sand is called a sand tray, and you can arrange the miniatures any way you want in the sand to show me what it is like for you to ruin your daughter's life.
Client:	Um, I guess I can do that. You want me to use those [points at the miniatures]?
Counselor:	Sure, any ones you like. You can't do this incorrectly because you are showing me your experience. Once you have shown me in the sand, it will help me understand better.
Client:	[Hesitantly] Okay, I'll try.

At this point, it is helpful to physically move your chair back to give clients space to think about what to do. Lean back and observe, but unless clients engage you, keep silent until they are finished. When they are finished, they will say so or look at you for guidance. Ask if there is anything they would like to add to their creation. This gives them the opportunity to add or change anything that they may have been considering. When they are satisfied, then ask them to tell you about it. While they explain their creative work, notice their body language, pauses and avoidances. Also notice key phrases, metaphors and vivid word choices. These are all hints. As they explain, reflect, but refrain from asking questions for the most part. You can come back and ask for clarification later, but the first time through, you want an uninterrupted overview of their personal experience. Figure 7.2 provides an overview of these steps.

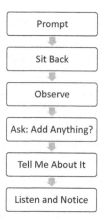

Figure 7.2 Basic Framework for Facilitating Creation

Skill: Silence

Sitting in silence is a basic counseling skill that is essential in the creation phase. The therapist is usually more uncomfortable in the silence than the client, who is focused on the creation. Therapists may be concerned that they should be *doing* something, unaware that what the client is doing is very important and words or actions could detract from the client's work. Instead, careful observation is exactly what the therapist needs to be doing.

At times, clients may be clearly frustrated with the creation or dislike what it shows. Resist rushing in to comfort or alleviate strong emotion. The client is moving into the next stage. Observe for indications that the client is shutting down or too overwhelmed (in other words, leaving the window of tolerance), but otherwise, give the client the space to bring those strong emotions into the present. Simply sit in the silence. This work is not verbal work.

How to Provide Enough Scaffolding for the Client

Scaffolding describes how educators help people learn in that sweet spot in education that is a challenging stretch, but not too difficult (Hammond & Gibbons, 2001). The metaphor of scaffolding provides a word picture for Vygotsky's concept of how, just as builders provide an essential but temporary support, teachers provide temporary support to assist learners to develop new understanding, new concepts and new abilities. That is exactly what you will be doing in the creation phase. You want to provide enough structure, or scaffolding, around the activity to support the client's ability to do it, but not so much that you make it too rigid with rules or so little that the client flounders trying to understand.

The first time you use a creative technique, many clients may be unsure about doing it right. In one grounded theory research study exploring child-centered expressive arts and play therapy, the researchers found that participants expressed initial insecurity about working with the art mediums, but overall considered it stress-relieving (Perryman et al., 2015). We see that a lot. Reassure clients that there is no right or wrong way to do it because they are showing you their own unique experience. That provides scaffolding by giving the client the self-direction to determine how they want to do it. However, note that this is important information for you. The client is revealing a desire to please you, to do the assignment perfectly, or to meet outside expectations. This is not enough information to completely determine, but it probably hints at a core need. For example, the client above may be struggling with the need for inner value, which she tries to meet through pleasing others. If so, her unspoken question is really, "Do I have value if I make a mistake?" When the counselor responds with, "You can't do this wrongly because you are showing me your experience. Once you have shown me, it will help me understand better," then the counselor is answering the unspoken question by addressing the core need of Inner Value while also expressing unconditional positive regard.

Once you have given the prompt, clarify as needed, but keep it succinct. You want to convey that the client decides how to do it. Some clients may need a few clarifications, but this is part of the work for them. Already they are showing you the experience of being them. Part of their experience interacting with the world is understanding the rules and expectations so they can do the right thing and meet those expectations. It is difficult to move forward with a task until they have that clarification. Again, if you have hints about a core need, respond in a way that addresses their need. Concerns about doing it right may indicate that clients derive their value from others' opinions, and they will often try very hard to please others to gain a version of that value. However, all clients are different and have different stories, so the same clarification questioning for another client might be about understanding limits and needing to know if it is safe enough to assert control in this new environment with you, a safety and security need. Regardless, they are already doing their work.

Some clients will be guarded about revealing too much. Expressive techniques may seem threatening because they feel too vulnerable. These clients may only use one or two pieces in their creations and talk in short, often one or two word, responses. This guardedness may indicate the core need for empowerment and control, and it may show itself as overly controlling or fearful of a lack of control. If so, address that need in your response. "It seems like it is important to you to protect yourself. In here, we don't have to talk about things that you don't want to talk about yet. Just tell me, 'I don't want to talk about that,' and we'll move to something else." With these clients, it is important to not offer too many insights, because that may seem scrutinizing. Also recognize that in creating a safe space, you may not use expressive techniques at all, certainly not until these clients are comfortable with the depth of that kind of work.

Other clients may not need clarification, but they freeze at the possibilities of a blank canvas. Allow them sufficient time to work through that, but when they seem genuinely stuck, pull back and process the here and now. "This seems hard for you, so let's pause for just a minute and tell me what is happening with you right now." You might ask what the client is thinking or feeling, or you might ask about the sensations they notice in their physical bodies. Keep it grounded in the moment right now. This will help you understand whether they are afraid, overwhelmed, or possibly dissociating. If a client needs to be more grounded in the present, then ask him to notice the red items in the room, the hum of the air conditioner or the sensation of the seat beneath him (as examples). Like above, this is the work, not the prelude to the work.

Creative Techniques: The Expressive Arts

Which expressive art form you use does not matter, so we suggest using the top two or three that seem to work well for you. Each medium has strengths and limitations, and you will learn different things about the client, depending on the ones you choose. However, the larger themes around core needs will surface regardless. It is best if you have additional training and knowledge in the ones you use. By using the ones that are comfortable for you, the therapist, rather than trying to find which one would work best with each client, you will become more confident at drawing on your professional intuition, which will guide this process. So, like your theoretical orientation, it should be based on the therapist's preferences, but implemented through a client-centered lens. However, by having two or three expressive art techniques from which to choose, if a client is averse to one expressive art, then you can easily shift to another.

Below are some ideas for prompts for each of the expressive arts listed in Chapter 2. Many of the prompts can be adapted for other expressive arts, but this gives you a sample of how you might use a prompt in the creative phase for three examples: exploring a label or diagnosis, understanding a key phrase about self, and gaining a broader understanding of family dynamics.

Art

"You've told me a lot about your eating disorder, but I think it would help me if you could show me what it is like to live with it. Could you draw (or paint or sculpt) me what that is like?"

"You said that you hide behind your smile a lot? I'd like to explore that more, that idea of hiding the real you. Show me that, if you would. You could fold a piece of paper in half and sketch a self-portrait for me of what others see on the outside and what you are really like on the inside of the paper. Then, together we can talk about it."

"I'd like to understand your place in your family, the people you live with right now. Would you paint a picture of your family members to help me understand what they are like?"

Drama

"I've heard you refer to your good side and bad side several times now. I'd like to understand how those two parts of you communicate with each other. I have these two chairs. Would you be willing to try a dialogue between your good side and your bad side so I can hear how they sound? The two chairs will help me see as you switch between them."

"That's a powerful word you just used to describe yourself. I wonder if you'd be willing to do an activity about that word? Write that word on the dry erase board, and then I'd like you deliver a monologue about it. You can use any props or costume that would be helpful to get you in character."

"I think it might help to do a family sculpture. I have this box of figures, people and animals. Would you arrange them on the table to show me your family?"

Dance and Movement

"So, you have been diagnosed with OCD. I would like to understand what your compulsions are like. Would you be willing to show me – using your body and motion – something that you need to do? I'd like you to physically exaggerate what it is like before you do it and what it is like after you do it. I want to understand your inner experience, not so much the specific action that you do."

"We have a confidential, enclosed space behind the office, and I thought it might be helpful to take it outside today. Are you game? We've got a basketball goal, so maybe we can shoot hoops today and talk about a phrase you used last week to describe yourself, the firework of the family."

"I'd like to try something creative to better understand how you see each one of your family members. Let's stand up. I'm going to say a name, and I'd like you to show me, as if your body were a statue, what that person is like. We might go through them a few times, so you can show me multiple characteristics of each person. Ready?"

Music

"You keep describing it as 'my anxiety.' It sounds like it is a part of you that is never separated. I'd like to hear what it feels like for you. Would you be willing to try something really different? I have this guitar, and I'd like you to make noise on it that sounds like the song, 'My Anxiety'."

"You said that you want to be invisible, yet here you are and your heart keeps beating. It's not silent. I wonder if we could use that idea of a beating heart and the bongos to hear what it sounds like to want to be invisible at school?... at home?... on the bus?... with your friends?... with your stepmom?..."

"The loss of your brother has had a big impact on the family. I wonder if there is a song in your playlist, or just one that you know, that captures what it has been like for you? We could listen to it together and maybe find the words online."

Photography

"You've been struggling with depression for several months. I have an assignment for next time. I don't usually give homework, but I think you might need a little time for this. Would you be willing to take about five photos on your phone that show me what your world is like when you feel this depression? We can talk about them next time we meet."

"A bleeding heart. That's what you said gets you into these toxic relationships. I wonder if you can show me what your bleeding heart looks like. You can use the photo editing app on this tablet to change the tone, distort, or add textures to a clipart of a heart or picture from the internet. Or, you can use several images and make a collage. Show me your bleeding heart."

"Thank you for bringing this picture of your family. Today, I thought we'd try an activity where you change this photo of smiling faces to reflect what your family is really like. You can use the scissors, colored paper, markers or anything else. Or we can do it digitally with photo editing software."

Sand

"There is a lot happening with this PTSD. How do you feel about touching sand?... It would help me to visualize your life with PTSD, and I think it might be helpful to you, too, to look at it from an outside perspective. You can use any of the miniatures on the shelves or anything else you like, and I'd like for you to show me your life with PTSD in the sand."

"You feel all alone in this. I wonder if you can show me that in the sand. What is it like for you to be all alone?"

"I want to understand your family dynamics better, so I'd like for you to create a family genogram in the sand, if you would. That means that I'd like to see your family tree and relationships. You can use any of the miniatures on the shelves to represent each person or pet in your family."

Writing

"This bipolar diagnosis has been challenging for you. I'd like to understand what it is like for you internally as you try to make sense of it. I have a container of writing instruments here and a few choices of paper there. If you'd be willing, I'd like you to spend two or three minutes free writing a letter to bipolar. Then, when you are finished, you can read it out loud to me and we'll talk about it."

"You said you don't really know who you are because you were adopted. That must be confusing. I wonder if you would be willing to try to write a poem for me to help me hear in your words what it is like to not know who you are. It can rhyme or not rhyme. It can follow a pattern or be free verse. That's all up to you."

"I have colored paper cut in squares and circles. I wonder if you would try a writing exercise with me? Pick a paper for each person in your family and write a description of them, including yourself, on each."

Skill: Professional Intuition

Some people are more intuitive than others, but we encourage students to develop what we call professional intuition. These are hunches, inspiration, and ideas that seem right, although you are not sure where they came from, combined with the knowledge from education, academic readings, and professional trainings. It is educated intuition, and therefore, it is usually trustworthy. When you know that blob in a piece of art is very important, but you do not yet understand why, that is your intuition based on what you know about art therapy and the client. When you notice a client flinch and you are aware when it happens again to begin to piece together a pattern, that is intuition informed by what you know about nonverbal communication. When you ask a seemingly unrelated question like, has something significant happened in a past September, that is professional intuition based on knowing that clients often have an escalation of symptoms around the anniversary of significant negative events.

In Creative Play Therapy, you are taking in lots of information from the client and filtering it through your professional intuition. When sitting with the client, try to simply be present with the client, not doing the analytical understanding that will come when you write your progress notes. To do this well, it will require leaning on your professional intuition without getting too much in your head following a formula or trying to get to a specific end point. This will guide you in knowing which prompt to provide, too. Learn to develop this professional intuition.

Prompts

This stage uses very short and simple prompts that invite clients to explore. The emphasis is less about the topic (which may not be the core issue) and more about the client "getting it out" in a tangible, external form. Toward the beginning of your working relationship, prompts may facilitate rapport building and the therapeutic relationship, but as you get deeper into the work, the prompts will facilitate core need work.

Begin by asking clients if they are willing to participate in the expressive art. For some clients, this may be uncomfortable. For example, I once had a client who repeatedly told me he could not draw when I suggested an art activity. I assured him that there was not a right or wrong way to do it and that I would not grade his work (this was in a school setting). Later, after multiple art activities, he drew an amazing piece of art showing his armor that he hid behind, and I was astonished at how skillfully he conveyed his experience. He then confessed that he had made an F in art class at his previous school because he did not complete assignments. I did not know that information, but it convinced him that he could not draw. Now, with more years of experience, I would have paused the first activity and processed it in the here and now before moving forward with art. That would have facilitated our relationship with more understanding, and the work would have moved quicker. Clients may be uncomfortable with the arts, guarded about revealing too much, or, like my client, having received messages that they are not good at them.

The creation is less important than the process. It is tempting, especially when first learning to use prompts to facilitate the creation phase, to focus on the product. However, the work is happening throughout the process, even if the client never actually gets to the creation. Some clients will not. If client seems resistant (see Chapter 13), that is the work. If a client struggles with how to start, that is her work. If a client starts, but gets frustrated and wads up his paper, that is the work. The creation phase is just a step in getting to the deeper work, but if the client has a need to resist the creation, it is likely that he also has a need to resist the deeper work or this is part of that client's process to get to the deeper work. Honor that because he knows himself better than you do.

All interpretation is avoided in this phase. When creating, clients are using their creative right hemisphere of the brain. That is why they often create in silence. Talking, analytical processes, or cognitive understanding will detract from their ability to be fully creative and unlock some of those guarded places.

Also, your interpretations of their experiences are presumptuous. You have not lived in their worlds. Your clients are the experts on themselves, and they will make meaning from their creations when they are ready for that meaning. However, your intuition, informed by your knowledge and training, will help you as you listen and respond as clients tell you about their creations.

The creation phase of Creative Play Therapy is where the work begins to take off. While shallow-level rapport building in the warm-up phase is necessary and part of the work leading up to the creation, when clients are ready, the expressive arts prompt deeper work. Though clients may use symbols and metaphors to express their inner experiences, it provides information that is tangible and concrete, an externalized version of their internal worlds.

From Skeptic to Believer: A Student's Story

First Name: Chuck
Age: 44

Sand? A bunch of toys? How can this possibly be called therapy? Admittedly, I was a complete skeptic when I first started courses in play therapy while pursuing my master's degree in clinical mental health counseling at Lipscomb University. Logically, I could deduce that children and adults could "loosen up" enough to talk about their trauma or problems by simply "playing with toys" (my uneducated description at the time), but I didn't have a clue about the underlying philosophies or clinical research behind the practice itself. Even during the learning phase, as opposed to the practicing phase, I could not visualize how the knowledge I'd obtained could play out, pun intended, as being a solid component of mental health counseling.

But I was willing to continue the journey. So, I packed my bag, both figuratively and literally. I filled it with white sand, action figures, stuffed creatures, little green army men, costumes, and a plethora of other childhood thingamabobs. With my adult classmates beside me, we marched into an intense few days of hands-on, experiential play therapy practice, under the guidance of our professor, Dr. Denis` Thomas.

I quickly realized the world I had just entered was not only free of virtually any rules, but it was also fun. Most importantly, it was safe. We began role-playing in teams of two, one as the client, one as the counselor. Out of sand and gizmos, one would construct a snapshot of whatever part of their lives they wanted to explore, while the other watched relatively silently, pointing out the many different choices, asking points of clarification, while mirroring back anything that was said out loud. Over and over we did this exercise, switching between client and counselor.

Everything began to click. This knowledge I had obtained in weeks prior began to marry with the actual experience of play therapy itself, producing the revelation that play therapy not only works, but it is a force to be acknowledged and pursued. I saw very quickly that the work has very little to do with listening, but everything to do with observing. "Interesting that the army men are guarding this particular wall." "Oh, that's your mother on the other side of this wall." "I see that you are nowhere in this sandbox."

In my experience, observing someone building and interacting with a world they create from scratch gives a different, and often a much deeper, insight into a person's psyche than one could ever glean from conventional analysis alone. And in the end, the whole experience of play therapy has been eye-opening and paradigm-shifting in a way that has made me a true and unwavering believer.

References

Etzi, J. (2004). Analysis of play. *The Humanistic Psychologist, 32*(Summer), 239–256.

Hammond, J., & Gibbons, P. (2001). *Scaffolding: Teaching and learning in language and literacy education.* J. Hammond (Ed.), Sydney: Primary English Teaching Association.

Kenney-Noziska, S. G., Schaefer, C. E., & Homeyer, L. E. (2012). Beyond directive or non-directive: Moving the conversation forward. *International Journal of Play Therapy, 21*(4), 244–252. doi:10.1037/a0028910

Perryman, K. L., Moss, R., & Cochran, K. (2015). Child-centered expressive arts and play therapy: School groups for at-risk adolescent girls. *International Journal of Play Therapy, 24*(4), 205–220. doi:10.1037/a0039764

Emotional Expression **8**

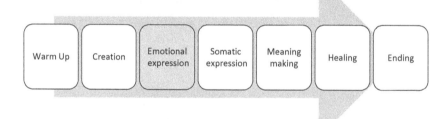

Figure 8.1 Stages of Creative Play Therapy

Once you have facilitated a safe space with empathy, genuineness and unconditional positive regard, clients can move into deeper creative work if they are ready and have the resources assembled around them to do the work. At some point, clients will naturally begin to explore closer and closer to core needs and move into the emotional expression stage. This stage is characterized by a welling up of strong, often surprising emotion. This may be witnessed with tears, rage, a need to physically move or stoic withdrawal. It generally is an intense version of how the client typically deals with emotion.

In the previous stage, clients used an expressive art to create a tangible product to show you their experience. Some clients may create a scene that is a concrete recreation of an incident or dream and others will create something more abstract. After the creation, ask them to tell you about it. In the beginning of their verbal explanations, you mostly use reflections to facilitate the telling of their stories. After clients have explained it to you, you will move into processing their story. Using your professional intuition about the important parts of their creation, informed by what you have noticed about what they emphasized or omitted, you facilitate moving the session into deeper content, and as you get close to core needs, a strong emotional expression occurs. The next section provides a framework for how to facilitate this. Keep in mind that each client is different, so adapt as necessary.

Counseling Skill: Holding Pain

We provide a holding place for the client's pain. Holding difficult content, shameful experiences and horrifying trauma is a skill. Most people are averse to this kind of hurt, and in trying to protect themselves, they shut down the person in pain, rejecting their experience and their emotions. When holding client pain, avoid rushing into problem solving. The pain does not stem from lack of solutions, and it must be felt to be relieved. Problem solving comes later. Also, while holding pain, the therapist does not need to soothe clients. Empathy, yes, but clients do not need the message that it is unacceptable to feel and show their pain. Soothing usually happens because the therapist is uncomfortable, so you want to keep the focus on the client, allow the raw pain to become visible.

How to Process the Creation

To process the creative work, first listen and reflect. Begin with an open-ended question or statement like, "Tell me about what you have created." While they tell you, use basic reflections and occasional reflections. During this portion, listen to the content, but also be aware of the nonverbal content. Clients will often talk about what is happening in the creation in the third person, so follow the client's cue and also use third person language. Identify things in the creation using the client's words and phrases. For example, if the client refers to something as the bad guy, use that phrase, not who you suspect it represents. Avoid interpretation.

Counseling Skill: Reflection

When using reflective responses during the creation phase, the therapist is reflecting the client's experience of her world, which may or may not be reality or truthful. It may feel awkward for a professional helper to say things out loud that are wrong or contrary to therapeutic values, but saying out loud what the client thinks and feels internally, especially when it is the client's distorted reality, can be powerful. Therefore, if a client says something when talking about herself like, "She was responsible for it. She made it happen," the helper would gently reflect that back. "It's her fault it happened." When this is especially unpalatable, you could also try using the third person distance with, "She believes it's her fault it happened," but use this judiciously, since it can come across as patronizing. The truth might be just the opposite, since, for example, a young child does not cause or invite abuse. However, what the therapist is doing is externalizing the inner experience, not validating it as truth. By saying out loud what the client has heard internally, it becomes possible to change it.

Below are five things to notice as clients explain their visual creations. (They might need to be changed or adapted for auditory creations.) While the client is telling you about the creation, refrain from sharing what you notice. You'll do that next, after they have explained the whole creation to you. For now, this is just the therapist taking note internally.

- Notice any differences in the order they created and the order they explained it to you.
- Notice anything that is part of the creation but that they do not explain, omissions.
- Notice overt discrepancies in how it appears and how it is described.
- Notice anything that seems to draw your attention as important and how the client explains it.
- Notice relationships of objects/representations, how close or distant, what emotions are associated with them, and size differences.

Second, comment on what you have noticed. Client creations are a vulnerable sharing of their inner world, so tread carefully here. Be cautious about presuming to know what it means. Meaning making comes later, and it will come from the client. You want to say something like, "I notice that your partner is twice the size of how you show yourself," not, "I can see that your partner dominates you." By noticing, you invite the client to agree, disagree or clarify. Sometimes, what seems glaringly obvious to you is simply the use of the tools available, and another characteristic was more important. This also helps you gently probe to draw insight and challenge the client while respecting the vulnerability of the client sharing his highly personal experience. If you notice something and the client says, "I don't know what that is," or a casual, "I just liked that," move on to the next thing you notice. Everything that is included serves a purpose, so even though the client may think at this point that it is not meaningful, it is. However, do not try to overvalue what the client does not.

Third, circle back to what you noticed that the client could not tell you about. I like to ask something like, "Tell me what you can about this," and purposefully parrot back the adjectives or phrases used to describe it. Come back and repeat this a few times as needed. Try something like, "I'm still curious about this."

Fourth, link things in the creation. You may draw attention to things that have been described or shown similarly or you may draw attention to things that are opposite. This is especially helpful with the unknown parts.

Finally, process the work in the here and now. Ask, "What was it like for you to show me that?" or "What was it like to see that from an outside view?" or "How was that, creating art and sharing it with me?" After a general overview, ask specifically about what is happening physiologically. "What are you feeling in your body right now?" If you did a body scan earlier with the client, follow up on previous sensations and compare those to now. It is very important to ground past trauma experiences with the present. When clients are processing childhood traumas, this allows them to bring the resources they have as adults to their work.

Once this creation has been processed, based on time, you may choose to prompt another creation that further explores the first one. You might want to take one aspect of the first creation and expand it or follow a theme that emerged.

Processing the Creation

1. Listen, reflect and notice.
2. Comment on what you notice.
3. Circle back to the unknown.
4. Link parts of the creation.
5. Process in the here and now.

Emotional Expression

Strong emotional expression happens when a client is in the right brain, so the welling up of strong emotion is not something that clients can usually wrap words around at the time. It is important that clients are able to feel the depth of the emotions that are swirling, so most of the time, you want to allow the space for it to be uncomfortable. The exception is when it becomes too overwhelming, retraumatizing, or the client dissociates. When that happens, pause in the work and do here and now processing, using closed (yes/no) questions to bring them back to the present. If the client is able and wants to, then go back to processing the creation. Pain is uncomfortable and this stage is about walking through that pain, not backing away from or blocking it. Raw pain is difficult for the therapist to witness, but it is the ultimate expression of unconditional positive regard. In this phase, clients are coming face to face with their deepest fears: What if my mom does not really love me? What if I will be alone forever? What if I will never be safe? What if this happens again? What if I am worthless/unlovable/cursed?

This stage is like lancing a boil. First, the emotions will bubble up, then, when they are released, it will gush forth and often get messy. Only after the wound is drained, does true healing occur. The therapist's goal in this process is to trust that a painful lancing of the wound is the way to healing and to not obstruct the process by preventing the full draining of emotion or soothing so that the lancing does not happen.

The most common emotional expression is crying. This may look like anything from shedding tears to great sobs welling up from sorrow, anger, isolation, unlovability and/or vulnerability. It is difficult to see a client reeling with this kind of pain without wanting to ease it, but for true healing to occur, sit quietly with it. It is intense, but usually fairly short in duration.

Generally, we see two kinds of crying responses. First, some clients show the intensity of the emotion externally. They will sob, the kind that makes it hard to catch your breath, that feels physically like your heart is breaking. These clients crumple before your eyes with the weight of it. The second kind of crying response is much more reserved. For some clients to cry at all may be very intense, yet it may outwardly look like just a few tears slipping from the eyes, usually in silence or just occasionally punctuated by a sob or moan.

Other clients may get very fidgety as strong emotion sizzles through their bodies. I prefer to remain quiet and let the client decide what to do with that most of the time, but I have fidget toys available and within reach. Rarely, I might set play dough in front of them or quietly suggest that we go for a walk if they are talking in this stage. These clients need to process the emotion with physical motion because they "feel" physically in their bodies and therefore need a physical release. More on that in the next chapter.

Some clients will rage. Sometimes, they use words or phrases, but sometimes it is through actions, like annihilating a tissue, tearing up their drawing or destroying their creation. For some clients, this may be the first time they have allowed themselves to feel anger toward a perpetrator or the situation, so anger may look different. One client described anger as "blue" and "cool" when at this point, but that beginning of expression is still intense and new.

Very occasionally, clients may curl up and withdraw with or without crying. They may cover up with a blanket, pull a pillow in front of them, or draw their knees up and hide their faces. They may turn away from you or crawl into a smaller space. Allow the emotional space for whatever response the client needs to feel deeply. These clients are comforting themselves and may have been rejected for visibly showing strong emotion in the past, so staying present and facing them is essential. This is not the same as clients who do not engage in the counseling process to protect themselves, because to be in this stage, they have already warmed up and moved through the creative process. They just need to pull back because they still fear being rejected or having their emotions dismissed. For these clients, it is important to support their emotional expression.

How the client shows emotion can differ widely, but the common theme in this stage of the counseling process is the intensity of it. As you reflect clients' inner fears, distorted truths and shameful beliefs, you externalize their internal experience, allowing it to be seen, heard and experienced differently. This also facilitates therapeutic work on past experiences with present resources. The closer you get to the core need, the deeper the emotional intensity around it.

In this phase, you want to facilitate the client safely experiencing the pain to move through it. You do not want the client to continue in a cycle of re-experiencing trauma without movement toward healing. In observing the client, watch for symptoms that the client is overwhelmed or dissociating from the pain. If this happens, return to the here and now and ground the client in the present. Many mindfulness techniques will help with this, but anything that requires the client to use their senses to be present in the current space and time works well. "Tap your toes slowly on the floor and notice the sensation." "Notice what you hear right now." "Look around the room for the color yellow, and know that you are safe."

According to Dr. Dean and Dr. Anne Ornish, making emotions known to yourself, recognizing them and sharing them helps decrease the emotions most commonly correlated with chronic diseases, such as isolation, anxiety, hostility, stress, depression and anger (Ornish & Ornish, 2019). If emotions are not expressed, they become trapped inside and even become debilitating to health. They include cultivating connections and support as part of their program to reverse chronic disease.

Counseling Skill: Sitting in the Stuck

The counseling skill of sitting with the client during the emotional expression phase is what we call *sitting in the stuck*. When clients feel deeply, it is difficult to talk. Sometimes, the situation feels hopeless and unchangeable at this stage. There may be grieving for what happened and what will never happen, and it feels immovable. As helpers, it is challenging for therapists to see such great pain in their clients and not *do* something. We chose this profession to help, after all, and sitting in silence seems unhelpful and disempowering. However, the most helpful and empowering thing to do, the thing that brings long-term relief, is to simply sit and be fully present. If a client sighs deeply, you might mirror that. You might gently say, "This is hard" or "It really hurts" or another reflective response, but use those sparingly. Silence is very powerful in this phase. The client is doing a tremendous amount of work, but most of it is inner work, so what they need is the space and safety to do it. You will process it later.

Prompts

Prompts and most words during emotional expression are avoided, unless initiated by the client.

Creative Techniques: Self Care and Mandalas

During this phase, the creative techniques used are the ones used during the creative expression phase, since this is an extension of the creation. However, this is a good place to mention the importance of self-care (see Chapter 15). As you become more proficient at Creative Play Therapy you will walk with clients through difficult content, raw pain, and your own personal reactions to those who inflicted pain. To have the capacity to remain present with your clients, to reflect back their distorted beliefs and to maintain unconditional positive regard, you must have self-care practices that allow you to be fully authentic. To sit in the stuck, you need to be psychologically healthy. Failing to do this will result in burnout, compassion fatigue and vicarious trauma.

Creative Technique to Try

We require our internship students to explore journaling through mandalas, and we have mandala journals, too. A reflective practice is important, and we want to teach them a creative option. Blank mandalas provide the option of journaling in a creative way that does not require writing (although it could certainly include words). Get a sketch book or blank journal and draw a circle that nearly fills the page. You can use a compass, bowl or template. Fill the blank circles with whatever images and colors you need. Add a title and the date to help you when you review them. Play music if you like. With the rise in popularity of the mandala coloring books, some people find it relaxing to color the templates provided. If you like that, do it and enjoy the benefits. However, templates do not provide the reflective practice of externalizing your personal experiences into a creative form like blank mandalas.

Case Study

First Name: Nala
Age: 25

One day something terrible happened. Something that would change the entire course of the rest of my life. I was a collegiate athlete experiencing the freedom that came with being a freshman at college. The freedom I felt was intoxicating. I was a first-generation college student with an athletic scholarship. But one day, one small moment changed all of that.

I had a seizure in my first week of college classes, and it was completely terrifying. I was shocked. I was embarrassed. I was shaken to my core. The body that once had earned me a scholarship was backfiring on me. I felt as if I had lost complete control. The nurse told me everything I should avoid and explained everything I should do to never have one again. This prompted the saga of panic attacks and extreme anxiety that crippled me for the following years to come.

I was so freaked out that it would happen again, so I stopped leaving my dorm room, stopped making friends. I became obsessive over the things that nurse had told me to do to avoid having a seizure ever again. I ate the "exact" balanced meals at the exact "right" time. I drank the exact amount of water my body was "supposed" to need. I became what I call an anxiety robot. I began to fear just about everything. I eventually dropped out of college and moved home. My life was crumbling before my very eyes. Everything I had worked so hard for was slowly falling away. One seizure. One traumatic event shook me to my core.

I was so afraid that it would happen again that I started to fear just about everything. I was too afraid to take a shower alone, for fear that I would fall and have a seizure and crack my skull open, so I took baths. But then I was too afraid I would have a seizure in the bath so I would have my mom sit in the bathroom while I was bathing. Before I knew it, my life became smaller and smaller by the second. I was a fragile shell of a human.

Fast forward, with my parents help, I was re-enrolled in school. I was suffering through daily panic attacks to attend class because it was important to my parents that I graduate from college. I left just about every class to run to the bathroom because I was hot, sweaty, and nauseous from panic that I was going to have a seizure again in front of everyone.

Eventually I began seeing a sports psychologist who saw how my symptoms affected my entire body. At the time I literally looked like a walking ball of anxiety and he suggested I try getting active again. I thought, no way. My problem was in my brain, not by body. Back then I did not understand how the human body can hold trauma and emotion. I couldn't see how my mental illness affected my body. My boyfriend at the time started running, and I tried it on the treadmill one day. I was shocked at how the feeling of running felt similar to the feeling of panic attack in my body. The only difference was that I consciously induced the feeling and then was able to feel it go back down. At the time I didn't realize that I was exposing myself to the somatic response that I feared so much. I just knew that I felt better after I ran, and I was quickly addicted. I didn't know why running helped but I knew it did. So, I just kept running. I craved it. One mile slowly became ten. Before I knew it, I was a runner. It wasn't about the distance. It wasn't about the sport. It wasn't about fitness. It was about feeling my heart rate rise to where it felt out of control and then recognizing that I could always bring it back down. I began processing this with my therapist and I still couldn't understand how it worked. I still had a lot of struggle and had to fight a tough battle to graduate college, and never did I think the day would come that I would live without panic and fear. I still didn't understand the connection between the two things that had healed me: therapy and movement.

Now I have to remember that sometimes talk therapy just doesn't cut it. Our bodies hold more than we are aware of and if you can allow it the freedom to release and express, they will begin to heal themselves. I thought I had lost my body that I once controlled but instead I gained a greater understanding of how this beautiful body of mine works. It worked for me and gave me my life back. I continue to run every day. It's my daily remembrance and practice of self-care. Never would I have thought that I would find meaning and gratitude for the seizure that once crippled me. But here I am, grateful as can be because I can now help heal others.

References

Ornish, D., & Ornish, A. (2019). *Undo it!: How simple lifestyle changes can reverse most chronic disease.* New York: Ballantine Books.

Somatic Expression 9

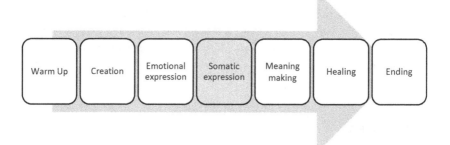

Figure 9.1 Stages of Creative Play Therapy

In the popular book, *The Body Keeps the Score*, van der Kolk (2014) made the argument that people hold trauma in the body physically. If there is a physiological component of trauma, then it makes sense that there is a physiological component to healing as well. We, too, noticed the phenomena that some clients had strong somatic reactions during intense work, often stronger than the emotional response, such as rashes, upset stomachs, vomiting, shortness of breath, gagging sensation in the throat, feeling cold or hot, and tingling in the hands, among others.

It may be that this stage is a sub stage of the emotional expression stage, since not all clients experience it. However, we have included it as its own stage because of the importance of the physical work that occurs. Clients that tend to physically experience things tend to have somatic responses in their work, too.

Understanding What Physical Sensation is Telling the Client

Physical sensations provide important clues about how the client is processing their work. For example, clients who have been overpowered and struggle with the core need of power and control, specifically needing to have a voice, often experience physical sensations in the throat area. Clients who feel burdened may feel a weight across their shoulders. Clients who experienced physical blows may feel tightness in the area where they were hurt.

Because the somatic sensation may have changed from the direct physical experience, adult clients may have gone years without linking the two experiences. Likewise, there may have been a gap in time between an event and when they experienced the somatic symptom. However, for other clients, the somatic feeling is a metaphor and not based on any true physical experiences. For those reasons, it is important to understand the client's experience of the somatic expression to better understand how the body is processing it.

We like to say that the body is sending a message. If the message is ignored, the symptoms will often increase, but once the client understands the message the body is physically sending, the need for that communication dissipates. This phase of the work is about understanding what the body is communicating to the client. As always, the therapist needs to be a keen observer. Notice signals of discomfort, such as fidgeting to get comfortable, rubbing a specific spot, stretching certain muscles, or facial winces. Clients tend to be unaware of these actions, so drawing attention to physical patterns is helpful to begin this phase. You could try something like the following.

Therapist: Ouch, you made a face that looks you are in pain. Tell me about that.
Client: Oh, it's just my elbow. It sometimes hurts from the accident.
Therapist: The car accident where you lost your daughter?
Client: Yeah. It's nothing. I was in a sling for a while, but it's not broken or anything.
Therapist: It might be nothing, but I'd like to explore that. What does it feel like?
Client: Feel like? I don't know. It hurts.

Therapist:	It hurts. And is that hurt a throbbing or a dull pain? Or something else?
Client:	Um, I guess it's a sudden pain that locks my elbow so I can't move it. It's not throbbing or dull. I feel a pressure that clamps it.
Therapist:	A pressure that clamps it so it can't move. When it can't move, is it in a certain position?
Client:	Like this. It's kind of an L shape.
Therapist:	You can't move it from that L shape.
Client:	Yes, but it isn't right by my side.
Therapist:	Where is it?
Client:	It's locked up here [lifts arm up in a flat L-shape with the elbow straight out to the side and fingers pointing forward].
Therapist:	And where is the clamping feeling?
Client:	It's pressure right here [points right above the elbow].
Therapist:	Does it have a temperature?
Client:	Now that you mention it, it feels hot, on my elbow and along the back of my arm.
Therapist:	Does it have a color?
Client:	Red. It's definitely red.
Therapist:	So, in your arm, you feel like something is clamping your elbow suddenly and with enough pressure to feel painful. It's hot and red.
Client:	Maybe it's less of a grabbing and more of a pressure along the back of my arm.
Therapist:	And is that what it always feels like, when you feel this pain in your arm?
Client:	Yeah, yeah, I just realized always just like that.
Therapist:	Okay, that's the pain in your arm. Now, I'd like for you to do a body scan.

Body Scan

To get a global understanding of what your client is experiencing, it is helpful to ask the client to scan their body for physical sensations. Some parts of the body are neutral, but some may feel intense sensation. Often, clients have two or three different areas that are signaling them, so I like to discuss each one separately. The first time you ask a client to do a body scan, it may be helpful to provide more structure, guiding clients through noticing each part of the body from feet to head (simply because most clients have fewer physical sensations in their lower extremities than their abdomen, chests and heads). On subsequent scans, you can just ask them to notice the sensations in their bodies as an abbreviated first step. Below is a step by step suggested approach.

First, ask the client to scan their entire body, from feet to head, and notice any physical sensations. This is a nice grounding technique for pulling the client into the here and now as well, but this first pass is internal and without verbal description. The client simply notices. You want to allow clients to inwardly learn to notice the body's signals, which will provide important information for them later as their body cues them in unique, but consistent, ways. For example, with repetition, clients will learn their own patterns of sensations such as, "That swirling feeling in my stomach usually means I am afraid of something. What do I fear right now?"

To continue the dialogue from above:

Therapist:	I'd like for you to do a body scan.
Client:	That sounds like an MRI or something.
Therapist:	No special equipment needed, though. Just sit up and relax for a minute. Take a deep breath, if it helps you relax ... Now, if you are willing, I'd like you to notice your toes and feet. Notice if you have any sensations, anything that feels tense, hot, cold, tingly or other sensations. Now notice your calves, observing the same sorts of things or anything unusual. Notice your thighs ... groin ... up your body through your abdomen ... chest ... down through the arms to the fingers ... back up to your shoulders and back ... neck ... face and head. Now, take another deep breath.

Second, ask clients to describe out loud what they noticed. Quietly listen for the overview without interruption. When they pause, prompt, "Anything else?" Keep a mental list of each one, usually about three to five different sensations, but, of course, it varies with each client and on different days.

Therapist:	Okay, now that you've noticed what your body is physically communicating with you. Tell me what you noticed.
Client:	Well. I still have that pain in my arm.
Therapist:	Anything else?
Client:	I have this swirling feeling in my stomach [swallows and grimaces]. It feels kind of nauseous [hugs abdomen].

Therapist:	Anything else?
Client:	I feel kind of shaky all over. And my eyes. They feel hot.
Therapist:	Shaky all over, hot eyes, anything else?
Client:	[pauses] No, I don't think so.

Third, ask the client to rate the intensity of the sensations in order. Which one feels the most intense? Next most intense? And so on. This helps you understand which information is the most important, what the body is communicating the loudest.

Therapist:	So, you noticed your arm [rubs the back of the arm mirroring client's previous action], your stomach [hugs abdomen], your eyes [touches the eye socket in front of temple] and feeling shaky all over. Would you rate those in order from the one that feels the strongest to you to the one that is the least noticeable?
Client:	Let's see … My arm hurts the most. Then, that swirling in my stomach. I feel like I might get sick.
Therapist:	[moves trash can near client] If you need this, that's okay. If at any point this starts to feel too intense, let me know, and we'll do some mindfulness techniques to help you stay right here and ease some of the symptoms. You can also hold this fidget toy [hands stress ball to the client], and when it feels like a lot in your body, notice the texture of this instead. How are you right now?
Client:	Okay. I think I'm fine right now.
Therapist:	Alright, your arm feels the most intense, then your stomach, what's next?
Client:	My eyes, then that shaky feeling.

Next, ask the client to describe again the most intense sensation. I usually start with the physical sensation the client rates as most intense because that is what the body is sending the strongest communication about, but if a client seems like that might be too much, you could try reverse order or start with the second most intense response. When in doubt, ask the client which seems the most important to talk about first.

A very important part of creating safety for the client is to provide emotional safety when processing somatic symptoms. Remind clients that they have permission to stop whenever they need. This is important for empowerment, especially for those who feel helpless. Periodically, and when the

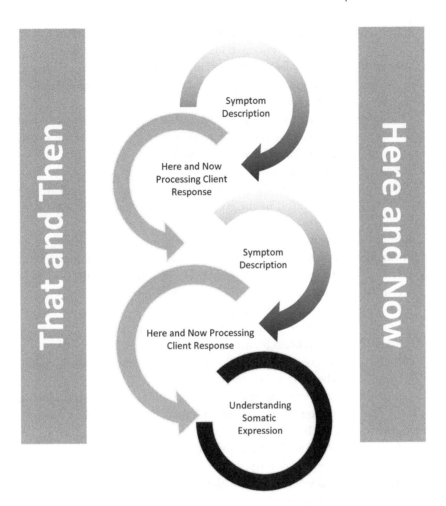

Figure 9.2 Somatic Expression Processing

description is intense, pull out of describing *that and then* and move to the *here and now*, the client's experience of describing it to you in your office. In addition to creating safety, a practical aspect of pausing the processing and moving to the here and now is that it often makes the symptoms more manageable and separates the past from the present by allowing the client to use current resources (like the therapist) that were not available previously.

> *Therapist:*   Let's start with your arm then. Would that be okay?
> *Client:*   [warily] I think so.
> *Therapist:*   You don't seem too sure about that. What are you thinking?

Client: I usually try to avoid thinking about it, so it seems weird to focus attention on it. I'm afraid maybe it will get worse.

Therapist: You usually avoid it, and the fear is that by thinking about it, it will get worse. My guess is that it is already bad enough.

Client: Right. I don't need it to get any worse.

Therapist: Thanks for telling me that. What if we proceed slowly and with caution then? If it starts to get worse, you let me know, and we can stop anytime you want.

Client: I think I can do that.

Therapist: I'll check in with you periodically to make sure it's okay with you, too. It might get uncomfortable, but I'll be right here with you.

Client: Okay.

Therapist: You told me earlier that you get a pain in your arm right at the back of the elbow. Describe that to me again.

Client: It's a hard pressure, like something is resisting it.

Therapist: Resisting it? Pushing on it?

Client: No, more like when you hit something solid.

Therapist: It feels like it hit something.

Client: Yes [repeating a motion moving her arm back and stopping, when it is in an L shape].

Therapist: You keep stopping when your arm is right there [mimics the motion]. Is that where something hits your arm?

Client: Yes, that's when it hurts.

Therapist: What is behind you that hits your arm?

Client: The back of the seat.

Therapist: And when your arm hits the back of the seat, it can't move. You said earlier it feels hot.

Client: Oh! [covering her eyes and beginning to weep]

Therapist: You just realized something important. How are you right now?

Client: I'm, I'm okay. I just realized that is what I did in the car accident.

Therapist: You said you are okay, but I want to check in and make sure. Do you feel ready to continue?

Client: Yes. I can continue [looks up at the therapist].

Therapist: That is what you did in the accident [makes the arm motion].

Client: I put my arm out to protect my daughter, but it hit the seat, and I couldn't hold her back.

Therapist: And it hurts right here [pointing above the elbow].

Client: I got a few stitches. But I didn't protect my daughter.

Therapist: Your arm is telling you that you didn't protect your daughter.

Finally, you label the somatic expression. It could be related to a specific event, like the example above, "Your arm is telling you that you didn't protect your daughter." It could be a warning of danger, a sensation that was felt anticipating a recurring trauma, "That sensation is telling you to get ready because something bad is going to happen. It is trying to protect you." It could even be a feeling following a trauma, such as the swirling stomach signaling fear. In the example of the mother in the scenario above, her stomach swirling sensation started when she feared something bad had happened to her daughter. That feeling was confirmed and then generalized to other fears. She now feels it when she feels any fear. While most somatic expressions seem to originate from trauma, some may be more general, such as holding stress in the shoulders.

Skillful Questioning

In traditional talk therapy, the skill of questioning is one of the most important. When exploring somatic expression, the therapist needs to ask good questions to decipher what the body is physically communicating. We teach two types of questions in our basic skills class: open-ended and closed questions. Open-ended questions invite the client to talk more, and closed questions can usually be answered with one word. Since this phase of creative play therapy is more directive and talk based, you will likely use both, but the best therapists use this kind of questioning strategically.

Skill: Open-Ended Questions

When you want to facilitate the client's free, uncensored thoughts, ask open-ended questions. These usually begin with *what* and *how*, such as, "What sensations did you notice?" or, "How does that feeling in your stomach physically feel?"

Open-ended questions are broad, and do not solicit specific types of information. They are helpful for gaining an overview and lots of pieces of information. Clients can answer these in multiple ways, and they generally talk in paragraphs when answering. Sometimes they require the client to think more deeply. Usually, we encourage students learning to become helpers to mostly ask open-ended questions, but there are times when closed questions are more strategic.

Helpful Open-Ended Questions to Understand Somatic Expression

- Help me understand that better. What is it like for you?
- How would you describe that feeling?
- If you were describing this as a symptom to a medical doctor, how you explain it?
- What does it physically feel like?
- When else have you felt this sensation?
- What does [a descriptive phrase the client used] mean to you?
- If this sensation had words, what would it be saying to you?

Skill: Closed Questions

When you want more specifics or a quick clarification, use closed questions. Closed questions require only a one or two-word response, such as a yes/no question or an either/or question. Closed questions are often used during intake interviews when you need specific information quickly without too many details. Closed questions also help provide clarification without expounding on a tangent.

In questioning about somatic symptoms, closed questions can be used to help clarify exactly what type of sensation the client is describing with a yes/no question such as, "Is it a painful feeling?" or an either/or question, such as, "Is it a sharp pain or a dull pain?" Sometimes, it is helpful to ask about the color or temperature of the sensation, which is not usually something the client would think to describe. That, too, is a strategic closed question that can be answered with a brief response.

You want to ask enough questions about the sensation to be able to nearly feel it yourself. If a client feels nauseous, is it a roiling feeling in the gastrointestinal area, a clenching of the stomach or an expanded gaseous feeling in the tummy? All may be described as nauseous, but it helps you to understand what the body is communicating. It is significant whether it is expanding (feeling bigger) or contracting (feeling smaller), as one may seem to demand to be noticed and one may seem to try to stay hidden and contained.

Of course, sometimes clients will provide more than one word to answer a closed question. They may provide more details or have an insight, and that is fine. The purpose is not to limit their answers in this phase, but to expedite the process.

Helpful Closed Questions to Understand Somatic Expression

- On a scale from 1 to 10, with 1 being low and 10 high, how would you rate the intensity of this feeling?
- On a scale from 1 to 10, how would you rate the discomfort of this feeling?
- Is it hot or cold?
- What color is it?
- Is it soft or hard?
- Does it have a sound?
- Does it have a smell?
- Is there movement with this sensation?
- Do you feel it on both sides of your body or just one side?

Physical Feelings and Metaphors

Some clients will naturally use a metaphor to explain somatic sensations. A metaphor (Metaphor, 2019) is a figure of speech where figurative language symbolically represents another thing, such as being so mad that you are a volcano about to explode. While not every client will use this literary device, when clients do, you can expand the metaphor by using related vocabulary, client phrasing and visual images to enhance understanding for both you and your client. Below is an example. Notice the open and closed questions as you read.

Therapist: Help me understand that better. What does the ache in your head feel like?

Client: I don't know exactly. It hurts.

Therapist: It hurts. What does that mean to you?

Client:	It feels kind of like an oil well pumping and drilling down into my brain.
Therapist:	So, it's like an oil well. Rhythmic, up and down, but not pounding?
Client:	Exactly. It's a constant up and down feeling.
Therapist:	What does the up part feel like?
Client:	It feels like anxiety. I know the drilling down is coming, but there is a slight pause first.
Therapist:	The up part feels like anxious anticipation. What about the down part?
Client:	That's when it drills down into my head telling me that I'm not good enough, that I deserve all this.
Therapist:	So the down part has a voice.
Client:	Yeah, and it's relentless.
Therapist:	A relentless voice. What does that relentless voice sound like?
Client:	It sounds like my Dad's voice.
Therapist:	Your Dad's voice drills down in your head telling you that you aren't good enough, that you deserve this. Sometimes, there is a pause, but even in the pause, you get anxious, knowing that it's just a matter of time until it starts drilling down again and again.

Skill: Empathic Listening without Judgment

Empathic listening is important throughout Creative Play Therapy, but the somatic expression phase may feel the riskiest for the client. If a client tends to have somatic symptoms, the body's way of physically communicating, it is likely that at some point he or she has been told that "It is all in your head," or "Just ignore it" or other insensitive and unhelpful messages, especially if the client has been to a medical professional and test results indicated that nothing was physically wrong. There may be a history with shame and embarrassment. For some clients, the physical sensations may be very disconnected from core needs and past trauma that the somatic symptoms are communicating about and thus seem to be unrelated to why they came to see you. If the client is skeptical, acknowledge the skepticism. If a client is hesitant, be willing to go slowly. If a client has strong physical reactions, look for ways to include physical movement in the healing process.

Prompts

Although we rarely prompt a creative activity in the somatic expression phase, we do tend to use three verbal starters to facilitate the processing. We like to use these to conceptualize left brain analytical processing, right brain creative processing and integrating both sides of the brain through Creative Play Therapy. The three starter phrases are:

Tell me.
Show me.
Help me understand.

Tell me. This starter phrase invites the client to give a verbal description of the somatic sensation. "Tell me what that tingling feels like." "Tell me where you feel that." "Tell me more about when you feel it." It changes a question into a statement, easing the interrogation feel of rapid questioning. However, it is closer to a demand than a question, so it will also be more directive. Tone of voice is important here, since it should be an invitation to share more, not a requirement. This is left hemisphere analytical processing, wrapping words around the experience.

Show me. We use this prompt often in the creative phase, but it can be useful here, especially when the client is struggling to explain what they are experiencing. "Show me the rhythm of your heart pounding." "Show me in exaggerated form what it feels like to have that weight on your back." "Show me how a panic attack starts." When clients use metaphor, they are attempting to show you their experience with a word picture. When invited to "show me," clients move from the left brain, analytical attempts to convey their experiences to the right brain, creative attempts, and, intentionally inviting the client to move between the two brain hemispheres promotes a physical as well as emotional healing.

Help me understand. I like this prompt because this work is a journey that requires both of you. The client does the work, but your experience and expertise with Creative Play Therapy guides the journey. In explaining their stories and experiences, clients are able to externalize them, reframe them, and heal from them. "Help me understand how the stomach tingling and the heart racing are related." "Help me understand exactly what that pounding on your right shoulder feels like." "I can see you just got some insight. Help me understand what just happened." This prompt begins to pull it together.

Creative Technique: Mirroring

Mirroring is a highly useful technique in the somatic expression phase. As you observe your client punctuate verbal descriptions with nonverbal actions, use the same motions with those phrases when reflecting back. Sometimes, it is helpful to use the motion instead of too many words. For example, if a client references a sports injury and says he feels a thumping in his knee, and as he says this, he holds his kneecap, lifts his leg, and moves his foot back and forth, then when you refer to that sensation, do that same motion. If he pairs an emotion with that sensation, then say the emotion while doing the motion. "Sometimes, you feel discouraged, like you are always held back from what you want," while holding your kneecap, lifting your leg, and moving your foot back and forth. Later, that becomes a shorthand. "Your sister's demands sound like this" while doing the motion to pair that sense of being acted upon by outside people and events to link two seemingly unrelated events.

Somatic expressions provide rich information about what the body is trying to communicate. By deciphering the messages, you and your clients bring to the surface what has been hidden. Not all clients express strong somatic responses, but those that do may also need a physical body movement release as well. Once you have gathered information and learned core needs, you are ready to make meaning from it.

Physical Cues: A Body's Way of Communicating

Name: Josh

My first experience with play therapy was during a 4-day intensive therapeutic experience which deeply shaped how I view play therapy and the power of the mind-body connection to this day as I navigated my experience of somatic expression.

Starting day two, I began to feel nauseated. By the afternoon, I had a notable, sharp pain near the top of my abdomen. It was mild enough to continue with little hindrance, but it was significant enough to quell my appetite for the next 24 hours. I chalked it up to living an unusual schedule for a few days and just feeling generally, emotionally raw. I thought little of it and simply waited for it to pass.

The next day, Dr. Denis' checked in with me during a lunch break and noted that my lunch was left untouched. I explained my low appetite and discomfort during the past day or so and I dismissed it. Astutely, Dr. Denis' encouraged me to not minimize my experience and, with permission, Dr. Denis' gently asked more questions about what I was feeling – where the pain was located, was the pain sharp or dull, if it felt familiar, etc. As she prompted me to think more on my body's experience, I quickly made a connection between the "work" I was doing during my sessions and what my body was experiencing. Unpacking my physical discomfort helped me notice how similar the pain was to the feeling I felt after being punched and beat-up by my childhood bullies. While processing my bullying experiences in play therapy, my body apparently had something to say – that my childhood experiences of being bullied still deeply hurt and affected me as an adult.

My second experience with somatic expression took place during another multi-day, intensive play therapy experience. The work that came out revolved around the death of a beloved mentor, 10 years prior. Nearly at the beginning of my work, I felt the muscles in the back of my neck tighten and remain in that state for the next day or so. It caused unusual headaches and no amount of massaging or reclining could relive the tightness. Learning from my first experience, I made a point to let Dr. Denis' know and resolved to listen to my body to determine what it was trying to tell me.

Eventually, my sand tray work revealed my body's message – that I held a deep fear that my late mentor would not be proud of who I had become since his passing, and this fear was holding me back from pursuing my full, actualized self. It was as if a hand had me by the back of the neck, severely squeezing, and preventing me from moving forward – almost like a kitten with a mother's mouth on the scruff of the neck. My therapist prompted me to say goodbye to my mentor using the sand tray – using it to show him how his influence has helped shape who I am today and that he can, indeed, be very proud. Once it was complete, I was astounded by how quickly my neck relaxed, as if the grip was released.

The lesson I learned through these two experiences is that the "mind-body connection" is not a myth or metaphor. During both events, my body was keenly aware of my emotional needs before I was and, in an extremely tangible and physical way, demanded my attention. Now, I make a point to regularly "check-in" to my body and listen to what it might be trying to say; it often knows more about me than I do.

References

Metaphor. (2019). In Merriam-Webster's collegiate dictionary. Retrieved from www.merriam-webster.com/dictionary/metaphor?src=search-dict-box.

van der Kolk, B. A. (2014). *The body keeps the score: Brain, mind, and body in the healing of trauma*. New York, NY: Viking.

Meaning Making 10

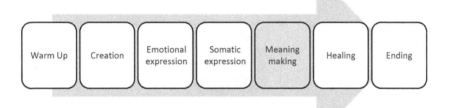

Figure 10.1   Stages of Creative Play Therapy

After you have spent time developing the therapeutic relationship in the warm-up phase, prompted a way for the client to externalize what is happening in the creation phase, maintained unconditional positive regard in the emotional expression phase, sought to understand what the body is physically communicating in the somatic expression phase, then it is finally time to pull all the information together into meaning making. Understanding what things mean is usually important for adolescents and adults, which is different than child play therapy. The work is happening, though, even if you do not understand what it means. Skipping the previous phases to get to understanding, however, will short-circuit the process. You need all the observations, information and creative work of the previous phases to be able to make accurate meaning from the work.

What Is Meaning Making?

Meaning making is the process of pulling everything together. By this point, you understand what resources the client has and is still lacking. You know the client's core needs. You have gathered lots of pieces of data from the creation phase, and you have learned how the emotions and physical body communicate with the client. You have noticed themes and repeated patterns in the client's work, and you probably have some idea about what elements of their work mean. You have observed how the client says things and the client's nonverbal language. You now combine that with all of your professional training and knowledge, along with your observations and the themes and patterns you have noticed, to make meaning from it. The core needs, resources, creation and expression will all come directly from your work in session with clients. The themes, patterns, observations and professional intuition are all analytically filtered through the therapist. The following figure provides a visual representation of the many factors that contribute to meaning making.

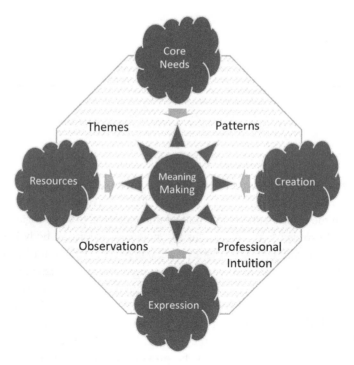

Figure 10.2 How to Make Meaning

Client Information

RESOURCES

In the Warm-Up phase, you formally and informally collected information about the client's resources: physical, mental, family, social, spiritual, creative, financial, personality, hobbies, etc. You know the client's preferred methods of coping, both helpful and hindering. You have determined where the client is with self-care.

CORE NEEDS

As you have proceeded through the previous four stages (Warm Up, Creation, Emotional Expression and Somatic Expression), you have pinpointed the core needs: safety and security, empowerment and control, inner value, and relationship. Because you have worked with your client for awhile by the time you get to meaning making, you know the areas where your client has unmet needs and how those core needs tend to be manifested.

CREATION

By this point you have at least one, and perhaps many, expressive creations that create a tangible product that you can both see, hear, touch and/or experience together, and you have discovered patterns. If you have more than one, even across mediums, you have noticed larger themes.

EXPRESSION

As the work intensified, you have witnessed how your client expresses strong emotion and how he or she senses it physically. You have learned more about what is demonstrated externally, and what is experienced internally.

Therapist Expertise

THEMES

As you work across multiple sessions and with multiple creations, you will begin to notice themes that emerge in the client's work. These are broad, overarching ideas that are consistent in the client's thinking, perception or understanding.

PATTERNS

Patterns often lead to themes, but may not be as global. You may simply notice that a client represented herself with a similar object as another session, linking the work from both sessions. Also significant is when a client deviates from a pattern.

OBSERVATIONS

You will continually gather observations as you work with clients. Some you will share with a client, some will wait until a later time to be shared, and some will remain private. Notice what is said and unsaid, shown and hidden. Observe body language and physical cues. Notice affect and any changes. Basically, you observe the entire session.

PROFESSIONAL INTUITION

These are your gut feelings, but they are informed by your education, supervision, continued learning, this book and other trainings. You are encouraged to trust this, and when in doubt, you can always ask the client.

What Is the Difference between Interpretation and Meaning Making?

When Dr. Kevin O'Connor, co-founder of the Association for Play Therapy (APT), spoke at the Tennessee APT conference in 2019, his presentation included a list of ways to interpret work. As a child-centered therapist, I (Dr. Denis') cringed at the concept of interpretation, and I still do. It seemed very presumptuous that I would know more about my client than my client. However, I could not deny as I learned more about his Ecosystemic Play Therapy treatment modality that I did most of the things he called interpretation. I suspect that the distinction is a small and insignificant one to this work, but the way I differentiate interpretation from meaning making is that it nearly always comes from the client. On occasion, I may tentatively suggest an interpretation based on professional intuition, but I generally try to keep meaning making in the client's words and preferably just from client's own conclusions. Still, I have experience with many clients, have been studying in this field for years, and I have learned much from my clients, so I notice things that could be considered interpretations. Also contrary to my client-centered roots, this phase is more directive. As professionals, it is important to learn from those further in this career, especially from those who practice differently, since it sharpens our own understanding. If this section seems like interpretation to you, I would agree that it leans in that direction. In this stage of Creative Play Therapy, we have grafted other theoretical approaches into our person-centered approach.

Why Wait to Make Meaning?

Each theoretical orientation determines the importance and order in which thoughts, feelings and behavior happen. Cognitive theorists believe that thoughts precede every action and emotion. Behavioral theorists believe that by addressing actions first, you can change behaviors, but also cognitions and emotions. Carl Rogers believed that emotions happened first, and they influenced thoughts and actions.

In Creative Play Therapy, we believe that feelings precede thoughts and behavior, although we freely admit that thoughts and behaviors also influence emotions. Emotions fluctuate, twist together, and sometimes swim in the places below our awareness. That can make them seem unpredictable and uncomfortable. However, emotions do not require action, simply acknowledgement. Therefore, the client needs to be able to feel and identify the feelings, and by doing so, change thoughts and behaviors. Changing thoughts and behaviors first can be helpful in relieving distress, but it does not provide the level of deep healing because it does not usually get to the core need that the emotions are trying to communicate. The previous phases facilitate the ways for the client to feel both emotionally and physically, even with emotions that have been blocked or unacknowledged. After the client has been able to feel the depth of the emotion, then it is time to use cognitive processes to begin to make sense of them in a more concrete way, the meaning-making phase.

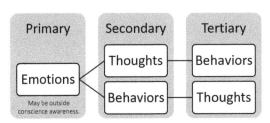

Figure 10.3   Feelings Precede Thoughts and Behaviors

Uncovering Patterns and Themes

In discovering patterns and themes, look for frequency and intensity. Patterns are usually first identified because they are repeated. "I noticed that you used the sky blue paint last week when you were talking about needing freedom. This week, you went for that color first again." It can be a repeated color, image, miniature, song or poetry lyric, phrase or dialogue during creation. Alternately, it can be a repeated feeling, topic or core need during expression. Intensity also cues you to be alert for patterns, vocalized phrases, or triggers. As you put these patterns together, you will begin to see themes.

Skill: I Wonder Statements

When you want to help provide the scaffolding for clients to interpret their own work, but you do not want to do the interpretation for them, "I wonder" statements work well. They offer a possible meaning or suggestion without requiring that clients agree with it. "I wonder if this poem that you titled 'Self-Doubt' is really about that need to be enough just as you are?" They may even sound like a question to prompt thought. "I wonder if not eating when you feel this anxiety is because you want to be smaller and take up less space, not be a bother?" Even if you are wrong, it allows the client to clarify.

When possible, pull together repeated themes across sessions and techniques. Look, too, for how the themes tie into core needs. As you begin to see the themes of how clients have attempted to meet core needs (and maybe in the attempt created more problems), together you and the client can address how to meet those needs in a healthier and more successful way. Encourage meaning making from the client's perspective.

Skill: Drawing from the Research

Evidence based practice is essential in the professional climate today, and it is good practice. While new, innovative ways to help the hurting are important, it is also important that practice is informed by the research. Those who tend to be more creative and more relational may cringe at the stereotype of number-crunching researchers in white lab coats. Yet, research helps us understand what works and why it works, so it is important to be aware. In addition, reading research may help with conceptualizing themes in your clients.

It is possible to review 50 journal articles a year by skim reading one a week, which takes about 15 minutes, depending on the article and how closely you read it. We encourage you to make an appointment on your calendar to steep your work in peer-reviewed empirical research. By the way, over 20 years, besides being more informed in your career and better able to identify themes with your clients, you would have learned from 1,000 journal articles (in play therapy). You might have referenced them with your colleagues and clients, informing others in the process, all in about 15 minutes a week.

Prompts

The meaning-making phase is more directive, but not specifically prompted. At times, you might explore a recurring theme by circling back and prompting another creation and moving through the phases again before coming back to the meaning-making phase. In this stage of Creative Play Therapy, instead of prompting a creation, you will help the client pull together resources, core needs, the creation, and what came up in the emotional and somatic expression into new meaning.

Creative Technique: And Then What?

As you are trying to uncover core needs, one technique that might be helpful is to repeatedly ask the client, "And then what?" Taking the client's answer, ask again, "And if that happened, then what?" With each answer, you get closer to the real fear, the real need that is unmet.

Client:	Every holiday I feel like I have to walk on eggshells so I don't upset my mom.
Therapist:	Upsetting your mom would be bad.
Client:	Oh, yes. That would be very bad.

Therapist:	What would happen if you didn't walk on eggshells and your mom got upset?
Client:	She would start yelling, and when mama's unhappy, we're all unhappy.
Therapist:	Let's say that happened, and she started yelling and you were unhappy. Then what?
Client:	I usually start to cry.
Therapist:	She's yelling. You are unhappy, and you start to cry. Then what?
Client:	She hates when I cry, and she usually tells me to dry it up or get out of her sight.
Therapist:	So, while you are crying, she is telling you that it is unacceptable, to dry it up or get out of her sight. Then what?
Client:	I have to leave because I can't stop crying.
Therapist:	You choose to leave. Then what?
Client:	I cry a lot because she doesn't love me.
Therapist:	You feel rejected by her when you cry, and that means she doesn't love you. Then what?
Client:	Well, I know she loves me, it's just ...
Therapist:	What if she doesn't love you? Then what?
Client:	Then no one will love me.
Therapist:	If your mother doesn't love you, then no one can love you, so it's better to walk on eggshells at all costs than feel like you can't ever be loved.
Client:	I never of thought of it like that, but pretty much. That's what it is like.
Therapist:	Now I understand why the holidays are so difficult. You either keep the peace at whatever cost to yourself or leave feeling completely unlovable. Neither is a good option. I wonder if there is another option, anything, that might be better?

Sometimes it is difficult to voice a client's deepest fear or we are quick to refute it. However, saying it out loud minimizes the control the fear has, and once it is spoken, you can work toward better solutions. Refuting the client's fear minimizes the client's experience and hinders the therapeutic relationship. It does not help the client feel better in the long run, but simply suppresses the feeling whether it is rational or not.

In the example above, it is possible that the mother really does not love the client. If that is the truth, then the client will need to learn to heal from that reality in a healthy way, so exploring the *and then what* is therapeutic. Saying it out loud may give the client the freedom to accept what is unacceptable. If the client is loved by her mother, but the relationship is dysfunctional, then directly verbalizing the client's fear – if her own mother cannot love her then no one can – brings to light a belief that is also dysfunctional and opens the opportunity to explore what it would be like if it were not true. As a third possibility, the client's fear may be untrue, and the client may know that it is really untrue cognitively, but the fear is causing action as if it were true, so it is still helpful to say the fear and the core need out loud, and say it directly. *And then what?*

Meaning making is a rewarding part of Creative Play Therapy because it pulls the loose ends of the previous stages together. It uses the therapist's analytical left brain and is the part where clients have powerful insights into what is happening deep within. This stage is where things begin to make sense, and it transforms difficult emotional expressions into healing, the next stage of Creative Play Therapy.

Healing 11

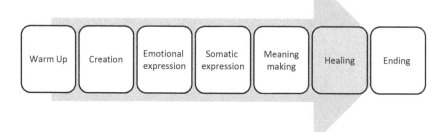

Figure 11.1 Stages of Creative Play Therapy

The healing phase of Creative Play Therapy is why we do this difficult work. We want to help clients heal from trauma, pain and suffering. We want to make a difference. We want them to experience joy again and be free from distressing symptoms, some for the first time in years. We want those who come to us for help to leave with a better quality of life. We want not just to help, but to heal.

For most of the clients you work with, you will see layers of healing, not an overall miracle cure that happens all at once. But as your clients experience micro healings session after session, they add up to significant life changes, and the more healing around core needs, the larger the impact of the improvement.

Pulling It All Together

Carl Rogers (1989) wrote, "This process involves several threads, separable at first, becoming more of a unity as the process continues" (p. 156). The healing stage is when you see the new tapestry that has been woven during the previous stages. As this stage is a review with clients, so it will also be a review now as we pull the threads together. Figure 11.2 demonstrates how the expressive arts, talk therapy, core needs and development combine with the stages of Creative Play Therapy to bring the client through the process and into the healing stage.

Revisiting Core Needs

Back in Chapter 4, you learned the four broad categories of core needs. Within each of those broad categories of core needs are some of the most common themes represented. The two foundational core need categories (safety and security, empowerment and control), just as in Maslow's hierarchy of needs, should be addressed first if there are multiple unmet core needs. The inner

Figure 11.2 Pulling It All Together

value core need will be most central to the client's being, and relational core needs are expressed in social relationships but may mask lower-level needs.

If a client struggles with meeting the core need of empowerment and control, and the therapeutic work includes role play on becoming more assertive in setting boundaries with a friend, that may be helpful, but it will not be healing. If instead, the work plunges to a deeper level of addressing the need for a voice that is heard, if the client physically feels in her throat the constriction of not having a voice, and if she learns with you to say things out loud that are uncomfortable, then instead of learning skills to use in one relationship situation, the client becomes empowered and believes that her voice deserves to be heard across relationships and situations. That is the difference between helping and healing.

Figure 11.3 provides a quick reference of the common themes for each core need.

Throughout the stages of Creative Play Therapy, listen and watch for unmet core needs. Clients may have a dominant core need, a cluster of themes under one core need, or multiple core needs with many themes. Also, a symptom may or may not fall neatly into a core need category. For example, disordered eating is a common theme under the empowerment and control core need, but, depending on the client's experiences, it could also stem from a client's safety and security core need.

Core needs and themes are always determined from the client's perspective.

You begin listening for unmet core needs from the very first session, but they generally emerge and become clearer when processing the creation. As you help clients become aware of their own core needs by saying them out loud and weaving together the threads of the need and the symptoms, you

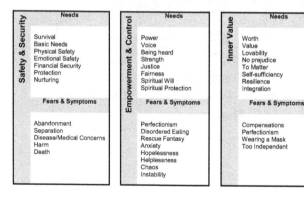

Safety & Security		Empowerment & Control		Inner Value		Relationship	
Needs		**Needs**		**Needs**		**Needs**	
	Survival		Power		Worth		Trust
	Basic Needs		Voice		Value		Intimacy
	Physical Safety		Being heard		Lovability		Attachment
	Emotional Safety		Strength		No prejudice		Committed Love
	Financial Security		Justice		To Matter		Honest Friendship
	Protection		Fairness		Self-sufficiency		Autonomy
	Nurturing		Spiritual Will		Resilience		Reparation
			Spiritual Protection		Integration		
Fears & Symptoms		**Fears & Symptoms**		**Fears & Symptoms**		**Fears & Symptoms**	
	Abandonment		Perfectionism		Compensations		Abandonment
	Separation		Disordered Eating		Perfectionism		Grief/ Loss
	Disease/Medical Concerns		Rescue Fantasy		Wearing a Mask		Isolation
	Harm		Anxiety		Too Independent		Shame
	Death		Hopelessness				Dependency
			Helplessness				
			Chaos				
			Instability				

Figure 11.3 Core Need Themes

will move into the two stages of expression. Often when you correctly reflect back a core need directly, it facilitates strong emotional expression.

Revisiting Emotional and Somatic Expression

Identifying and recognizing unmet core needs aloud to a client often releases a powerful expressive response. Some clients have both strong emotional and somatic responses, and some have one or the other. These two stages allow the client the space to completely feel previously forbidden feelings and hear what the body is telling them while grounded in the present in a safe environment.

After you and your clients have worked through the emotional expression and somatic expression phases, it helps to review where they were before feeling and where they are now.

- "Remember at the beginning when you said that it felt like you had swallowed bricks. What is that physical sensation like now?"
- "Before you said it was at an 8 in intensity. How would you rate the intensity now?"
- "That was extremely difficult to hear and admit. Now that you've sat with it for a bit, what does it feel like now?"

As you ask, listen for expressions of relief, lowered intensity and less fear. If you are not hearing that, continue to process the expression while mindfully staying in the present. Scaling questions are one helpful way to quantify this and give you a gauge to determine progress. As you begin to label and understand the emotions and the body's communication, you link emotion, core needs and the fears and symptoms to meet those needs and begin to make meaning from them.

Revisiting Meaning Making

After clients have externalized their internal world through creation and expressed and felt emotions and physical sensations, they are ready to understand what it all means. Be cautious about rushing to meaning making because missing the information in the expressive stages will limit the number of threads that you have to weave together. Some clients will begin meaning making in previous stages as they recognize what symbols and figures mean and discern why they did what they did in the creation phase. Some of the meanings will be clear from the beginning.

Sometimes, however, clients will say something like, "I don't know what that is," as they are describing an aspect of the creation. That is a clue of something important that is not yet at a level of awareness. It may be a complex emotion or tangle of emotions, something that is considered unacceptable, or something that they have not had the resources to deal with up to this point. The important thing is that they cannot name it or describe it very well, yet they chose to include it, so it is important. As you process the creation and progress through the stages, you will probably come back to it repeatedly, learning more with each pass.

Listen for adjectives, emotion words and gender pronouns (if it is a person) and parrot those back to the client. Also look and listen for that symbol's relationship to other things the client has represented. Notice clients' desires around that symbol. Do they want it closer or further away or completely removed? Consider if the symbol is part of the past, present or future. When unsure, gently ask clients directly. They may not be able to fully answer yet, but often they can give you more clues.

The meaning-making stage makes clear the unmet core needs and attempts to meet those needs, and uncovers the why behind the behaviors. Symptoms (and diagnoses) start to make sense in the context of attempting to meet needs. Clarity around situations clears shrouded shame and blame perceptions, and clients can begin to see these situations more objectively.

In this stage, nothing about client experiences has changed, but often a shift and reframing of the situation does. Emotions are recognized and understood, which changes cognitions, which leads to changes in behavior. This is how global healing happens, not just situation-specific helping. The emotional changes tend to be difficult to describe because they are right-brained changes. The cognitions that change are more left-brained, and integrating both brings physiological healing.

Skill: Affirmation

Affirmation is different from cheerleading. When cheerleading, you want to pump up other people, help them feel strong and yell, "Great job!" While helpful at sporting events, cheerleading is problematic in therapy. Cheerleading sets an expectation, and if clients want to please you, they will do more of that (or less if they desire to displease you). It is not client-directed.

Affirmation, on the other hand, affirms the person, not the action. It allows the client to swim in water with scary, undefined emotion, without cheerleading pressuring them to be successful. The swim may not feel successful at all, but more like drowning. Affirmation is an expression of unconditional positive regard.

Affirmation: You like that better.
Cheerleading: I like that.
Affirmation: You did difficult work today. I know it was hard, but you did what you needed to do.
Cheerleading: That was hard, but you did it! Way to go! Pat yourself on the back.

Cycling Through the Stages

Each client will progress differently, and the Creative Play Therapy approach allows for plenty of flexibility. Because it is client-centered, the client decides whether to lean toward talk therapy or do much of the work in silence. The therapist offers prompts, giving the client full autonomy to determine how to do them ... or even if the prompt is used. Given the variability between clients, below is a sample of how the stages of Creative Play Therapy might look with a client over five sessions using art and sand tray expressive arts.

Session 1

Stages of Creative Play Therapy: Warm Up and Creation

The session begins with introductions and small talk to build rapport and to begin to get to know each other. Using the intake form as a starting place, the therapist reviews stated reasons for therapy and any pressing concerns and safety needs, noting any areas where there seem to be a lack of resources. The therapist also asks about current resources that are helpful and notes areas of strength. To introduce expressive art into the session, the therapist prompts a self-portrait technique to learn how the client sees herself. Begin informally assessing for core needs.

In this example, the client, Raven, has recently given birth to her first child (a daughter) and is struggling with post-partum depression. She is a single mother, but has an on again/off again relationship with the baby's father. Currently, they are back together. She lists her mom and sister as resources along with a few close friends. She lacks financial resources and is not involved in a spiritual community. It is undetermined yet if her boyfriend is a resource. In her self-portrait, she shows herself as "sad and tired" and while she drew the baby, she is not holding her in the self-portrait.

The therapist notes that Raven has had a significant physical event (childbirth) and has a conflicted intimate relationship that lacks stability. She identified mostly females as resources. Even though Raven's affect is somewhat flat, she is able to articulate well. One area of concern is a possible lack of bonding with her daughter, but this is just a hunch (professional intuition) at this point. The therapist would like more information about Raven's relationships with her daughter and her boyfriend.

Session 2

Stages of Creative Play Therapy: Warm Up and Creation

After a few minutes of warm-up talk, the therapist asks about how the post-partum depression has been. Raven reports that it has been worse. She had a very difficult time motivating herself to even leave the house today, and probably would not have made her appointment had her mother not insisted and kept the baby. The therapist introduces sand tray, and Raven agrees to try it. "Show me what your post-partum depression is like for you," prompts the therapist. "There is no right or wrong since it's your experience."

Raven spends time in silence sitting and looking around at the miniatures from the couch. "You seem to be considering how to do this," says the therapist.

"I'm just having trouble getting myself up off the couch," says Raven. She slowly stands up and walks to the shelves. She puts a large whale with an open mouth facing the center of the tray. She puts a young woman in the center of the tray, in front of the whale's mouth with a baby at her feet. She considers for a moment and then adds a Dalmatian dog, a windmill and a cake in a cluster on one side and a brown disc and a clock on the other side of the tray. After looking at it, she nods. "Is there anything else you would like to add?" asks the therapist. "I don't think so," says Raven.

Raven explains the tray. The whale is the post-partum depression that feels like it is going to swallow her. She is the woman in front of it, and the baby is her child. The dog is her mother, "my watchdog," the windmill is her sister "who blows life into me," and the cake is her "sweet" best friend.

"Your watchdog mother helped you get here today," reflects the therapist.

Raven continues to explain that the brown disc is her boyfriend. "He doesn't do much but work, always punching the clock." She sighs and says, "This depression separates me from the things I like and the things I want to do with my life." She tells the therapist that she'd like to go back to school and do something with graphic design, but she can't now that she has the baby.

Session 3

Stages of Creative Play Therapy: Warm Up, Creation, Emotional Expression

Raven reports that the post-partum depression has been better this week. She has been able to clean the house and do some laundry, but she still feels exhausted. The therapist prompts, "Show me what it is like to be a mom" to better understand the relationship with her daughter.

This time Raven puts the whale on the side of the tray with the mouth facing the woman. The woman is facing the baby, who is in the middle, and on the opposite side of the tray she puts a small tiger. Then, she sprinkles paperclips around the tray. After looking it over, she adds some colored rocks. She explains that the depression dominates her day, and she feels like she is just one step ahead of being swallowed. Everything is about the baby, who Raven is quick to say she loves and would not give up, but the depression has taken over her life. The baby has created distance between her boyfriend and Raven. "All he does is work, which is good because it pays the bills, but we've lost us. He is usually a kitty cat, but sometimes he growls, like this week about cleaning the house."

The paperclips reminded her of diapers, but she finds bright spots in motherhood (the colored rocks). At this, she begins to tear up.

"Being a mom is hard," says the therapist. "It has completely changed the focus of your life, putting this little girl in the middle of everything. While she's a precious addition to your family, it moved you [points to the woman] and your boyfriend [points to the tiger] out of the middle and in opposite directions. It's not about you two anymore. I noticed that you started to feel something when you talked about the bright spots. Tell me about that."

Raven says that she wants to focus on the positive, but it is so hard. She feels like she is losing herself.

Session 4

Stages of Creative Play Therapy: Creation, Emotional Expression and Somatic Expression

This week Raven reported that the depression was about the same. She had a couple of really bad days, but the others were okay. She defined really bad as "I can't get myself to do anything except what is absolutely necessary. I took care of the baby. She's good. But I didn't get out of pajamas all day, and I didn't eat until my sister brought dinner over."

"Last week, you said you wanted to focus on the positive, the bright spots, but you felt like you were losing yourself. Can you show me that in the sand?" prompted the therapist. When Raven grimaced, the therapist said, "You just made a face. Tell me what you were just thinking when I gave that prompt."

"Oh, I just, I don't know," she said as she wiggled, like she was trying to shake something off. When prompted to do a body scan, Raven reported a pressing sensation on her shoulders and a tingling on the back of her neck. "That's just what I feel like when I'm stressed."

"So, you've felt that pressing and tingling before. Can you describe another time when you felt that?" Raven described feeling it when she learned she was pregnant. She was applying to college for the third time then, "but something always gets in the way."

Raven put the colored rocks in the sand, sprinkling sand over them to partially cover them. She then put a woman with her arms outstretched, reaching towards the rocks, on the opposite side. She put the baby on top of one rock, the tiger on top of another rock and a paintbrush on top of a third rock. "These are my bright spots, but they also seem out of reach. I really love my daughter. My boyfriend and I want to get married. And this paintbrush is my dream of graphic design. I'm pretty good at art." Begins tearing up again. "But with my daughter, I got this horrible depression. My boyfriend says he wants to get married, but he also says he isn't sure. And I can't seem to get to school to get the degree I need to get a job in graphic design."

Session 5

Stages of Creative Play Therapy: Creation, Emotional Expression, Somatic Expression and Meaning Making

The therapist began by reviewing the previous creations.

In the first week, you drew a self-portrait where you were sad and tired with a baby to care for, but not one you were enjoying snuggling with, one of the bright spots of a baby. Then, you created a sand tray with that whale breathing down your neck and about to swallow you with your mom, sister and friend helping you on one side, and your boyfriend on the other. He was kind of neutral. Hmm. That whale seemed to relate to those physical sensations you described, the pressure in your shoulders and tingling on the back of your neck. Next, you showed me what it was like to be a mom, and it looked pretty isolating, with the baby in the middle of everything and you far away from your boyfriend. That was also the week when you said that you managed to have the energy to clean the house, and that he growled about the house. You managed to overcome some of the fatigue to ease things with him. That mattered more. And last week you showed me how you have bright spots, but the bright spots as you really want them seem just out of reach, especially a happy family with your boyfriend and daughter, along with a fulfilling career in graphic design. That's discouraging. This week, I thought we'd change things up and go back to the art supplies and explore what you want in the future.

Raven showed more excitement than previously, and selected a black permanent marker to draw a caricature of herself at graduation holding hands with her boyfriend and daughter with a group of people cheering for her – her family and friends. After a second prompt to consider further in the future, she drew herself at a computer with a diploma on the wall and photos of her husband, daughter and son.

"I wonder what keeps this from being reality?" asked the therapist.

Raven massaged the back of her neck and stretched her shoulders. "I don't have a son, for one."

The therapist asked questions about the physical sensations Raven was experiencing when asked about what prevented her from achieving those bright spots. "Something always prevents it," Raven said. "What prevents it?" asked the therapist. "I do. I'm not good enough."

Together, they uncovered Raven's inner value core need. Raven explained that the post-partum depression kept her from being a good mom. She did not feel like she was good enough for boyfriend, and that is why he had doubts about marrying her. She did not believe she was good enough to get into college, and even if she did, she probably would not be able to find a job with other, more talented people, applying.

"What would it be like if you were good enough?"

"I could do anything," replied Raven.

"What does that tingling on the back of your neck and that pressure on your shoulders feel like when you say that?"

"It's almost completely gone."

They spent the rest of session talking about things that might help to remove the whale and other things out of sight behind the neck. One was to look back. Raven realized that her mom also had regrets about never going to college, and Raven felt like she had been the baby that prevented her mom's education. She now saw the cycle repeating. Also, her dad left the family when Raven and her sister were little, and Raven believed it was because of her. With a young baby of her own, she feared that her boyfriend would also leave, and she realized she was withdrawing as if he already had.

By the end of the session, Raven said the tingling on the back of her neck and the pressure in her shoulders was gone. When asked for three words that described how she felt right now, Raven said, "Hopeful, relieved and stronger." In follow up, Raven also said the post-partum depression lifted and she and her boyfriend seemed to be reconnecting, but she was not sure what was different. She no longer feared returning to work full time in a few weeks after her maternity leave, and she had already visited web sites of local universities to gather information on degrees in graphic design and art.

Creative Technique: Containing the Concern until Later

Preparing for transition to life outside your office can be challenging after an intense session, especially one that has cycled from creation to meaning making all in one session. A client's head may be spinning from the new connections they have made. They may be metaphorically gasping for air after a deep plunge. Therefore, you need to be skilled in facilitating that transition to leave at the end of an intense session.

First, begin transitioning early enough to allow time to walk the client through what it will be like on the other side of the office door. Five minutes is usually sufficient after the first time with a client, but the first time needs closer to 10 minutes. If you have not finished processing the creation or expressive responses, you might need to pause and start again by asking the client to recreate the creation in the next session. Notice anything that is different between the two.

Second, ground the client in the here and now. You might say something like,

> As we begin to transition into you walking out that door, I want to make sure you are ready to do that. If you would, put both feet on

the floor, sit up straight, and take a deep breath. I want you to notice something in this room. Notice the color and texture. Notice if has a temperature. Does it make any sounds? Now, take another deep breath. How are you right now in this moment?

Third, ask the client what he or she needs. Begin by asking clients what will happen right after they leave. Start with exiting your office and getting in their car (or walking to the next place) and find out what the rest of the day holds. Then ask, "Before you leave the office, what do you need or need to do?" For example, a client who has been crying may want to reapply her make up. Can she do that in your office or would she rather go to the restroom? If she needs some time alone, will she stay in her car, go for a walk, or go home? Most often, clients have a desire to withdraw and think (maybe writing or painting) after an intense session, but some clients may need to be around people. How will they make it happen?

Fourth, determine what happens after dark. Night time is when nightmares disturb sleep, loneliness gives empty hugs, and daytime coping strategies may fall flat. Ask about living conditions and what it will be like to be home tonight in light of what happened in the session. Differentiate strategies that give clients the ability to continue meaning making, with those that only offer escapism. Watching five hours of movies while stuffing emotions back down with food is clearly counterproductive to the work done. You want clients to learn to feel without becoming overwhelmed with emotions, but also accepting that they may not be ready to change all their unhealthy coping strategies immediately.

Finally, be attuned to any physical or emotional safety concerns. Clients may leave a session feeling raw, but they should also feel safe and cared for by the therapist. Wounds should not be exposed, and clients should be able to function at work, school or home after the session or arrange to be in a space where they can.

One client, who had experienced complex traumas, arranged her schedule to have the afternoon off after our sessions so she could have several hours alone before needing to be around others. During that time, she chose to write, listen to music, or take a nap before resuming her regular responsibilities. Together, we helped her decide what she needed and needed to avoid. She needed time to be creative, the opposite of her analytical work, and be alone to recharge her introverted self. She needed to avoid people, work demands and anything physically taxing. This helped lessen any fears around what would happen when the therapist was not around, too.

Prompts

One of the most common prompts for the healing stage is a mindfulness prompt to ensure that the client is grounded in the present and preparing to transition. These can be short and quick. Scaling questions and other quantifiable prompts are also helpful to informally determine change and distress levels.

Another type of prompt to transition from a creation about the past or fears about the future into the here and now present is to ask about the experience today with Creative Play Therapy.

- "What was that like for you?"
- "What was it like to show me what happened?"
- "What was it like to finally say that out loud?"

Prompts in this stage concern connection. Their purpose is to link information and connect the client with concrete experiences from the past while firmly standing in the present with all the resources available now. Healing prompts are about being in the present.

Healing: Grief and Identity

Age: 23

My experience with adult play therapy was emotionally draining, powerful and utterly transformative. I had eight sessions in three days, during which I worked on two separate issues: grief after the loss of a close family member, and a damaged self-identity.

I expected to spend all three days working through my grief, but was surprised by how rapidly I made progress. By the end of day one I felt as though I had been able to say goodbye to my loved one, and bring some level of closure to the loss. For seven months I had been devastated by this loss, and in one day I felt reoriented and more at peace than I had since she had passed away. I had watched her be buried at her funeral, but at that point I will still caught up in the whirlwind of planning a funeral, and it was all still too raw. However, getting to bury her with the miniatures and supplies was oddly freeing. I was able to leave pieces of myself with her through symbols represented by the miniatures, which enabled me to feel as though I could move on without the guilt of letting her go.

However, once I had dealt with the grief, I was left glaring at a problem I have struggled with for years: my identity. I had been living in an existential agony for so long I didn't think I would find a solution. Being different isn't easy when you live in a world trying to make you like everybody else, especially when you throw in religion and a people-pleasing personality. I was damaged and fragile, too afraid to live into myself. I have spent several years in talk therapy working on this issue, and yet I made more progress in those few days of play therapy than I did in all of those years.

What made the experience so powerful and transformative was that I didn't just feel my emotions; I saw them in front of me, represented by the miniatures I was using. Given autonomy by my therapist, I uncovered emotions I had never been able to label or understand; I also connected these emotions to the figures in my story in a way I had never been able to before. At times it felt overwhelming, but I felt empowered to know I was in control. I was in control of what happened in this story unfolding in front of me. For so long, I had felt as though I could not control my emotions but through the visual acting out of the story with miniatures I was able to work through and reclaim my emotions.

In the beginning I felt shame looking at the damaged person I was left with after letting others define me. This shame quickly turned to anger; an anger toward those who had taken it upon themselves to label me (an anger I had been holding onto for a long time). This anger culminated in me frantically scrawling an expletive-centered phrase directed at those who had hurt me. After I finished writing, I felt release followed by panic (I realized my therapist was right there, another person saw me say that about someone else!). I looked up to see an expression of understanding and acceptance. She accepted my anger, and gave me a voice that I was never given in real life to act out what I needed to say. I reclaimed my voice, and experienced a surrender of that anger which has not resurfaced since.

Over the final few sessions, a sense of peace grew within me. I was given a platform to work through complex emotions, and grow in understanding of who I am (not who other people tell me I am). I left my final session with a stronger sense of self, an increased confidence, closure to grief and to the hurts of my past. In being given the freedom to authentically exist, the toys revealed myself to me. It truly was one of the most impactful and transformative few days I have experienced.

Play is a human experience, not a child's experience! The social constructs of the world tell us that play is for children, but I truly believe inside each of us is a child longing to play with freedom (we simply aren't provided a space to act on this outside of play therapy).

Since being a client in adult play therapy I have not found myself re-experiencing the problems I had before. The positive effects it had on me have remained, and my life is easier because of it. Whenever a thought creeps in questioning my grief process, or my identity, I look back at the photos I took of my play at the end of the final session and I am reminded of the truth the play therapy process revealed to me. Having the memory of a visual image, something tangible, has been very beneficial in terms of serving as a reminder of healing.

References

Rogers, C. R. (1989). *On becoming a person*. New York: Houghton Mifflin.

Ending

12

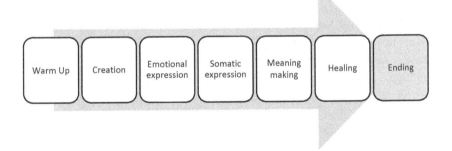

Figure 12.1 Stages of Creative Play Therapy

When you work with clients through the healing process, it may be difficult to end the therapeutic relationship … for both of you. You have shared something deeply meaningful, possibly life-changing, and both therapist and client are impacted by the work. This will not be a simple goodbye.

The Therapist's Ending

Before talking about ending the relationship from the client's perspective, which is essential in a client-centered approach, it is important to pause and recognize that the therapist will have a response to the ending, too. Using Creative Play Therapy, the therapist's reaction is often, "This was one of my favorite clients!" Obviously, they cannot all be favorites, yet we develop such an abiding sense of unconditional positive regard for the client in front of us, that this one feels like a favorite, maybe *the* favorite.

Together, you and your clients will share raw, poignant times together. You will be the only person on the planet who has witnessed the externalizing of this client's private world. You were the one who heard, saw and felt the deep pain of an unmet core need. Yet, you were also the privileged person who was an eyewitness to the reframing of the pain as the client wove together the pieces of his story into the tapestry of meaning making. You saw hope dawn. Shifts seemed to spontaneously happen outside the office, and brokenness healed into strength. You were vested in this relationship, and your skills cultivated the space for this work to happen. You have likely cheered the victories and felt the disappointment of setbacks along the way. Now, it is ending, and you may never see or hear from this client again. The two of you have been on a very special journey together, and it would be inauthentic to consider ending that journey without considering the therapist's reaction to the end.

When we teach counseling skills, we encourage students to consider how they like endings. Some like to linger and savor, possibly keeping mementos. Some like a short, sweet ending without much emotion. Still others like ceremony and celebration. Pause for a moment and consider how you prefer endings.

- How did you celebrate a university graduation?
- What do you do at the end of a semester or your child's school year?
- What do you do at the end of a moving movie?
- How do prefer to grieve the death of a loved one?

As you answer these questions, you will uncover some patterns about how you like to end. I (Dr. Denis') love the anticipation of endings. I tend to count down weeks and days until big events. I often find a final celebration of an accomplishment, like graduation, to be enjoyable, but anticlimactic, and I often leave quickly with a contented sigh to avoid lingering on the ending. As an optimist, I prefer to dwell on to the positive, so I skirt the sadness when possible, and I have learned that lingering at these events increases the chance that I will leave feeling sad and wistful instead of content and nostalgic. I finish semesters (ideally) with a tidying ritual so that I can start fresh the next semester. I want as much as possible finished, packed away and cleared to make room for new things. I appreciate clear endings that clearly mark a semester or project as finished. Ambiguous endings are unsatisfying for me. At the end of a moving movie, I like to watch the credits until the very end, sitting in the dark sorting through my private thoughts and emotions. If I have been crying, I like that time to dry my tears and wipe my eyes, while the theater clears. I enjoy considering what made it a good movie, and noticing songs and locations in the credits. On the way out, I like to toss my trash, visit the restroom, and then reenter the outside world (my clean up ritual). When it comes to grieving loved ones, some of the same patterns emerge. I prefer to keep the sadness to myself (or at times a few trustworthy friends), and I do not keep very many reminders. Those mementos I treasure make me smile – remembering the positive and releasing the sadness. Mementos are very significant to me, but usually are not obvious in meaning to others. After deaths, I prefer to tidy up, take care of the details and get things put away quickly so I can clear the space to grieve privately.

When it comes to ending therapeutic relationships, I know that understanding these patterns is important. For the most successful endings for me, I do not linger on the loss of getting to work with this client or get emotional in front of others. I like to revisit the significant breakthroughs, recognize the growth and change and affirm the difficult work clients accomplished. I like to count down to the final session, both for preparation and anticipation, but I tend to find the actual end a bit anticlimactic. I keep treasured mementos from clients, but they are rarely clear in meaning to others. It is important for me to clean up and clear out progress notes, client files and calendar spaces. However, I have to be cautious about treating a last session like a checklist, making sure I have clearly prepared a client for next steps (my therapeutic tidying up), but losing some of my warmth and empathy. Some of my worst sessions have been leading up to endings because I have this tendency to shift into task mode. I have learned from my mistakes to be especially self-aware during this stage of Creative Play Therapy.

While these are Dr. Denis's preferences, other therapists approach endings quite differently. Some like to create keepsakes with clients (both for the therapist and the client). Some journal to capture their own emotional responses, keeping the confidentiality of the client, of course. Some have ending rituals or ceremonies and even call the end graduation. What are your preferences?

We are not always able to facilitate endings the way that we want, but understanding your preferences helps you consider what you, the therapist, need. It is also important to stay aware of when your preferences may be problematic. What would help you facilitate an ending that is satisfying and leaves you with a sense of job well done?

The Client's Ending

Now that we have acknowledged and embraced the therapist's response, it is time to consider how clients respond to ending the relationship. This special relationship is one of a kind for clients, too. Your clients let you into their private worlds, a place that even an intimate partner has not seen, and this relationship is extremely intimate, so even a positive ending will mean a loss.

You are the skilled helper that created a place safe enough to explore their deepest needs, biggest fears and rawest pain, and you are likely the only person on the planet that they would allow into that complex mess. They showed you, and only you, their private world, and some of it was so private that at the time, they may not have even been fully aware of what they were allowing you to see. You were the one who witnessed the deep pain of an unmet core need, the shame that drove unhealthy behaviors, and the unspeakable parts of their life. But, you were also the only person who truly understood the transformation of that tangled mess into something meaningful, something that transcended any type of explanation, no matter how eloquently they tried to share it. They knew they could trust you to cheer their victories, but they also knew that you felt the disappointment of setbacks, while never being disappointed in them, along the way. Now, while proud of their work and ready to stand on their own, they know that this kind of relationship probably will never be replicated, and if all goes well, they may never see you again. Their ending will recognize this special journey together, but also express a natural grief for the loss of an experience and a relationship that they may never experience again.

Ending this relationship prepares clients for what happens next and what to do if they need therapeutic services again in the future. It needs to blend celebration with loss, accomplishment with grief, and goodbye to your work together with a hello to the next step of the journey. Most importantly, the ending needs to honor both of your needs and preferences for closing this relationship positively.

How to Get to "The End"

Ending the relationship well requires preparation, determining what will happen next, and creating a contingency for returning to therapeutic work. These may be done over several months, several weeks or several days, depending on the setting where you work, client needs, and the circumstances around the ending. You may develop a pattern for endings that helps you to facilitate this last stage of Creative Play Therapy, but maintain flexibility since each client will be different. However, by this stage, you know your client well.

Preparation and Anticipation

First, you need to determine when to end. Many factors contribute to this. Sometimes, the ending comes at a natural break in the calendar or school year. Sometimes, the ending happens because one of you is transitioning through something like a move, new baby, or job change. Sometimes, factors such as third-party payers or other stakeholders determine that it is time. Ideally, you both recognize that this layer of work is complete, and the client does not need services anymore. Whatever the circumstances that determine the ending, you and the client will need to determine when the last session will be.

Working at a university counseling center, we had natural ending times at the end of the fall and spring semesters. Even with long-term clients, we would generally begin a semester with a conversation about what clients would like to work on and what they would like to accomplish during that block of time, about 100 days. This already sets up some sort of time frame for termination (a terrible word for ending), but one that is adaptable to change. Some therapists work in 12-week (three-month) blocks of time in a similar way.

As the time to end approaches, you might revisit client readiness to end a few weeks out. We like to do that as we are warming up at the beginning of a session. Starting with about three sessions remaining, begin to count down with the client. By giving the client three weeks to anticipate a clear ending, you have the opportunity to process various responses to the ending (yours and theirs). This also helps as they are packing up their work. Clients will naturally pull up to a shallower level in the content and intensity of their work in preparation for ending. If a client dives deeper into content or intensity, that may be a cue that the client is not yet ready to end.

Learn How the Client Prefers to End

Because you have a history of working together, you probably already know if this client needs extra time to anticipate a change, is stoic or expressive, or has a sentimental desire to capture reminders. It may still be helpful to ask the client, and you can ask the four questions I asked you above (or an adapted version) to begin to identify the client's preferences. Once you know your preferences and the client's preferences, facilitate an ending that works well for both of you.

Together, determine how you will use the remaining time. If you have three sessions left, what is most important to do? If neither of you expressed a fondness for keepsakes, then spending time creating a scrapbook of the drawings the client created may not be good use of time, but perhaps creating one new art collage from significant scraps of the previous art would review the journey well while at the same time letting the client decide what to do with the accumulated art pieces.

As part of reviewing the work, determine with clients if they accomplished their treatment goals. Did your work address the presenting issue from the intake interview? Are there things around treatment goals that the client is still concerned about or that do not feel completely resolved? Also, consider your therapeutic process goals, such as creating a good therapeutic working alliance or moving through the stages of Creative Play Therapy.

> **Past, Present and Future**
>
> You want to facilitate a look back, a present assessment and a plan for the future. First, review your journey together, including significant breakthroughs. Second, assess current resources and client confidence to progress without this therapeutic relationship. Finally, anticipate for future needs and plan how to return to therapy, if needed.

Determine What Happens Next

As you prepare clients to proceed without the safety net of seeing you regularly, review their resources with them: physical, mental, family, social, spiritual, creative, financial, personality, hobbies, etc. You will likely have visited these multiple times, so you probably are both aware of areas of strength and areas that could use some reinforcement.

You know now what the client's core needs are, and the themes that express those needs. While it is unlikely that those needs will disappear, the maladaptive behaviors around meeting those needs will. Ending is a good time to teach the client anything that has been evident to you, but may still be hidden to the client. It is also a good time to review how together you uncovered these needs and what you have learned about them.

If you have a client who expresses emotions somatically, then ending is also the time to do a somatic expression review. You want clients to become self-aware of how their bodies physically communicate with them. Since this is less understood in Western cultures, it is helpful to directly say what you know. If a client has vivid nightmares that you have processed in sessions and uncovered patterns around, then going forward, you can remind him that nightmares are, for example, a creeping fear of unsuspectingly seeing a perpetrator again. He can then ask himself, "What is prompting this fear now?" Or if a client has a physical feeling in her shoulders that she has now identified with fear, then she can use it as a cue to ask, "What am I afraid of right now?" Going forward, the client now has the skill to decipher what the body is trying to communicate.

Creating a Contingency

While clients at the end of your therapeutic relationship may be doing well now, in the future, they may need or want services again. Ending is a good time to consider what to do when that happens. This is challenging because many things could change by then. Maybe you will be working elsewhere. Maybe the client has moved to a new community. Maybe some specific concerns that are beyond your expertise surface.

First, be honest. Do not make commitments that you may not keep or promise things beyond your control. Certainly, you want to let clients know how they can contact you and share your consultation policy and what they need to do to begin services again, if it is probable that you will be available. If you are a student, pre-licensed, have a partner in the military, or otherwise anticipate not being at this location long-term, be honest with the client about that, too, or speak in hypotheticals.

Second, inform the client about how to come back into services with you or someone else. If they come back to your agency, how can they request you? If they come back to your agency and you are not there, how can they find another good therapist? If they have to start fresh looking for a therapist in a different community, where would they look?

Third, consider times when the client might expect to need services again. Keeping in mind the development of clients, some of those milestones might also trigger new layers of work. For example, when working with survivors of child sexual trauma, common times when new layers of work surface could be when they become sexually active, get married, have children, and have children at the age they were when the trauma occurred. By discussing this at the ending, it normalizes the need, and by anticipating it, the client will not be as blindsided, confused or feel like a failure when it happens. This preparation is another way to shore up their resources, allowing them to be proactive instead of reactive.

Finally, when the ending is not ideal, you have an opportunity to model adaptability. Occasionally, clients will end services because of financial challenges, parent decisions, or partner pressure. At times, outside changes happen quickly, and it impacts therapeutic work. Do your best to review the past work, consider the present resources and confidence of the client, and prepare for future therapeutic services, even if you are faced with an abrupt last session.

It may be that your client does not like creative work, is not ready to do the work that is surfacing, or does not like you, and decides to end your work together. Listen without becoming defensive for any feedback that you can apply to become better. Know that sometimes you receive a reaction that is not about you at all, so maintain unconditional positive regard. If your personalities are not a good mix, then offer the client the option of transferring to a colleague, if that is an option. No therapy is perfect for every client, no therapist is perfect for every client, and Creative Play Therapy is not perfect for every client. This is why we need diverse therapists and treatment modalities.

Determining Client Readiness to End

While many factors outside of client readiness impact the decision to end, we want to end this chapter with how to decide when the client is ready. Ideally, this is a joint decision between you and the client, and the big question becomes when to end. You can tell when a client is ready by evidence of healing, consistently shallow depth of work, and client confidence to not be in therapy.

The first cue that it is time to end is that you see evidence of healing that has transferred to situations outside the office. What they came to see you about is not a problem anymore. Symptoms are gone, because the need for them is gone. The client is doing positive things that could not be imagined before. You may also notice a radiance in their faces and hear expressions of contentment.

The second cue that it may be time to end is consistent shallower work that is more aimless. When clients are deeply working, they are generally quieter, more intense, and highly focused. When the work is done, they talk more, are more relaxed, and less focused. While Creative Play Therapy cycles through different depths of work, and you often see shallower work between stages, you are looking for an absence of deep work. When sessions are consistently at a shallower depth, the client is generally done with therapeutic work (unless a temporary situation limits resources to be able to do deep work). Clients know their situations better than anyone, and they can be trusted to know when their overall work with you is done. This is different than working through a significant core need, keeping it shallow for a few sessions while experiencing healing, and then diving deep into another layer of core need. After multiple cycles, the work stays at a shallow level when a client is ready to end therapy.

A third cue that it is time to end is the client's confidence to continue without services. Sometimes, the client will express the desire to try it on their own. Other times, the client likes the safety net of seeing you consistently, even after the deep work is done. These clients may need a little longer to become confident that they can return when needed, and it may help to taper off services more gradually.

Skill: Trust

Clients trust you to move through the stages of Creative Play Therapy. The ending stage may require you to be aware of trust again. For some clients, you believing that they can continue on their own is a critical first step for them to believe it for themselves. However, to earn that trust, you must be trustworthy. Never promise, soothe or cheerlead to try to make the client feel better. Be honest. If a client fears what will happen if therapy ends, then cycle back and do a creation to explore that fear. Maybe what they fear will happen. What then? The fear is pointing to a core need that is not yet resolved. As you honestly process their fears, hear their core needs and affirm their progress, clients gain confidence about ending.

In the ideal scenario, you and the client see evidence of healing in behaviors outside the office. The work is shallow, comfortable, yet it may be aimless. Plus, the client is ready to end. Much variance exists across clients, but often progressing to ending happens much quicker than traditional therapy.

Creative Technique: Recollection and Mementos

When ending, most creative techniques are about recollection, not creation. All throughout the process, expressive arts creations may produce a lasting, tangible product that the client can reflect on at any time during the client's progression or regression (Perryman et al., 2015). At the end, however, these mementos may be especially poignant. One idea is to create a scrapbook to collect creations (or pictures or symbols of creations) documenting the client's journey. This gives the client a memento of the work with you, but also a reminder of how they were able to successfully navigate it before when core needs resurface in the future. This is a great ending exercise because it naturally allows you to point out patterns and affirm the client's work, while reviewing how far the client has progressed.

Prompts

The prompts for this stage of Creative Play Therapy do three things:

1. Review the Past
2. Assess Present Resources and Confidence
3. Plan for the Future.

You could prompt a creation (which will likely be shallower in depth than past creations) for these three things, or it might just be a verbal conversation. In those cases, you might start with 'Show me … .' Prompts help keep it client-centered, rather than you waxing into a long monologue.

"We've been working together for eight months now. I'd like you to create a timeline and show me the significant points for you in our work together."

"As we talk about ending our time together, I see a little hesitancy. Would you show me what your confidence is like about ending?"

"Looking ahead, what do you think things will be like in the future?"

Endings, like every other stage of Creative Play Therapy, are intentional. They are centered on the clients' experiences, but in this stage, you prepare for both you and your clients' ending preferences. This stage reviews the progress of clients, assesses their resources and confidence to end, and prepares them for future needs. Endings are a loss, so it is appropriate to express grieving, even while celebrating the difficult work it took to get here.

References

Perryman, K. L., Moss, R., & Cochran, K. (2015). Child-centered expressive arts and play therapy: School groups for at-risk adolescent girls. *International Journal of Play Therapy*, 24(4), 205–220. Retrieved from http://search.ebscohost.com/login.aspx?direct=true&AuthType=shib&db=pdh&AN=2015-43879-003&site=ehost-live&custid=s8863735.

Part III

Additional Aspects of Creative Play Therapy

In Part 1, we reviewed the broader fields of play therapy and expressive arts. We delved into active listening, core needs and an understanding of development. In Part 2, we outlined each of the seven stages of Creative Play Therapy, including creative techniques and prompts. Now, in Part 3, we turn to three additional topics.

First, we reframe client resistance as an active part of client work. Second, we explore spiritual concerns and existential questions. Finally, we conclude with practical ways to implement self-care using creative strategies. By the time you finish this book, it is our aim that you have a comprehensive treatment modality for an effective and rewarding approach to working with your clients.

Reevaluating Resistance 13

The literature in the helping fields often reports on the challenges of working with resistant clients. Much of it paints the clients as at fault, reassuring helpers that some clients just do not want to be helped. The clients, they say, are the ones who are challenging, withdrawn, disengaged and oppositional.

What if instead, resistance was a symptom, an attempt to meet core needs, too?

Take for example a 15-year-old girl, Su, who refused to see her therapist. Recently released from juvenile detention, mandatory counseling was part of her sentence. She had been doing well, and in the previous session she had a breakthrough, so the therapist believed they had made progress. Today, however, Su refused to enter the office. She was adamantly resistant. Switch to the client's perspective, though, and this resistant behavior makes more sense. The last session went deep, and Su revealed more information than she intended to the therapist. Six months earlier, she had trusted a social worker with her experimentation using and selling her parents' drugs, and that landed her in juvenile detention, removed from her family. She learned from that experience that people who appeared to care had the power to separate her from her family against her will, so she hardened her resolve to never let that happen again. Family always came first. The last session terrified her because she had shared information that she intended to keep hidden. Doing that could, from Su's perspective, cost her living with her family, and the risk was too great.

Consider the 13-year-old, Bella, who brought a book to sessions and read, refusing to even look at the therapist during every session. Not knowing what to do, the therapist offered her a choice. "We can either talk or I will go work on some paperwork until you are ready to talk." Three sessions later, Bella had still not spoken to the therapist. Switching perspective, Bella was caught in the middle of her parents' divorce. She did not want to live with her mother or her father, but with an aunt, but other people made decisions about where she would live and how long she would visit. No one listened to her. Even when her parents, the lawyer, or the judge asked her what she wanted and she told them, no one listened to her. The therapist was yet another adult trying to get information from her that her parents could use in custody hearings, which did not consider Bella at all. As a result, Bella determined that she would not cooperate any longer. She had control over what she said, and she would keep herself from giving any ammunition to her parents by reading a book.

Finally, consider Lee, a 37-year-old man whose wife gave him an ultimatum: get counseling and end an affair or she would leave. Lee loved his wife and wanted to save his marriage, so he agreed to counseling. Lee was verbally eloquent and persuasive. He was engaged and pleasant at the beginning. Yet, each time the session began to go deeper, Lee became visibly uncomfortable and shut down, so while Lee was coming to counseling as his wife requested, he was not making progress. Switching perspective once again, Lee's passive resistance becomes clearer. Lee valued his family and truly desired to stay married. After his own parents' divorce, he determined that he would make his marriage work. He equated divorce with failure, but deep down, he also believed that he would end up divorced like his parents. He also believed that it would be his fault. Lee hated conflict, and he felt it in his stomach, so he was a peacemaker. He always had a stash of antacids on hand. He was having an affair with his coworker that his wife knew about, but he also had engaged in two other affairs that she did not. He knew that if his marriage was salvageable, he would have to tell his wife about the other affairs, but even thinking about that had him reaching for the chalky tablets to settle his stomach. He avoided emotion and tried to keep things pleasant. His life seemed to be unraveling, and he felt powerless to stop it. He wanted the therapist to help, but whenever the acids in his stomach churned, he would do anything to make it stop. Shutting down worked and calmed the stomach storms.

These are only three examples. Resistance may look like aggression, irritation, opposition, anger, passivity, disengagement or stoicism. However, resistance is almost always an attempt to be safe and protected, regardless of the cost. It expresses a core need, but identifying additional core needs may require some digging. Start with safety and security.

Why Do Clients Need to Resist?

In the examples above, Su feared being removed from her family again, and she had good reason for her fear. Her parents still actively sold drugs, and she knew that one time of being caught would involve children's services, juvenile court or prison. She believed she needed stability at home, relationships with her parents, and protection of her family from outside agencies more than any benefits she might see from therapy, mandated or not. Her core needs were Safety and Security, Power and Control and Relationship needs. Bella, on the other hand, was most concerned about self-protection. She had been deeply hurt by both parents, and she could not trust them to provide her basic needs, so she grew up quickly, depending only on herself. Other adults also let her down, proving to her that they could not be trusted either, not teachers, not the judge, and certainly not this therapist. Her obvious core needs were Safety and Security along with Power and Control (needing a voice). A less obvious core need was for Inner Value. Lee also needed emotional safety, something he could not remember ever experiencing. When his parents fought, he quenched his own emotions to make peace, but he failed (from his perspective) and his parents divorced anyway. He struggled constantly with the volatility of emotions, but he has decades of experience quenching them, often with antacids. He needs safety to express his true self, something he seeks in extramarital affairs, so his core needs are Safety and Security and Inner Value. Peace in the moment is costing him what he really wants, a stable family that loves him unconditionally. He has relationship core needs as well, but the core need work that impacts his relationships the most are the lower-level needs.

Su, Bella and Lee are all trying to meet their core needs. Su is protecting herself from any threat to her family, freedom and basic survival needs. Bella is protecting her inner self and exerting her need for control in the limited way she can. Lee is running from emotions and the identity of being a failure, but in trying to make peace for others, he does not acknowledge who he is.

While their actions may seem counter-productive to what they really need, it works at some level to protect them. Su is not removed from her home, Bella does not allow another adult to disappoint and hurt her, and Lee can blame his future divorce on himself, sparing others from that blame.

Resistance, then, is protection.

How Is Resistance Part of the Work?

When clients resist work, that resistance is part of their work. Even if it were possible to go around the resistance, you would not want to do that, because working through the reasons for the resistance is important work and important to the work that comes next. Therefore, when you sense resistance in a client, pause the processing and move to the here and now. "Tell me what is going on with you right now." You can create safety in the present that you cannot in the past or future, so start there.

Use the skills from Warm Up to create safety, with a special emphasis on genuineness, empathy and unconditional positive regard. Express an understanding that the client is trying to protect himself, and that he probably has good reason to do it. But do not make promises that you cannot keep. In the example of Su, you may be legally and ethically bound to call children's services if you learn that her parents are actively cooking meth, even if it ruins your therapeutic relationship, because she is endangered. Most times, be clear before information is revealed (in the moment) reminding her that you have a legal obligation to report, giving Su the choice about what she reveals. This creates safety and trustworthiness, even if you do need to file a report.

On the other hand, if Lee discloses his multiple affairs, that information is safe with you, along with his shame, unworthiness, or other emotions he might reveal. When Lee changes from comfortably conversing to shutting down, explore what is happening internally right then. With Lee, a body scan would be very informative because, although he is shutting down on the outside, his stomach is churning and sending him strong signals internally. Lee needs affirmation that he can feel (physically and emotionally) safe with you without immediately trying to soothe the discomfort.

Bella, and other resistant clients who refuse to engage, will require creativity on your part. Ask yourself, "What is the why behind the behavior?" and then try to meet that need. For Bella, she does not trust that adults will help her, and she will not engage until she believes that the therapist is at least somewhat trustworthy and helpful. While she will not engage, she is listening, so this may be a rare case when you do most of the talking. "I wonder what I would do if my parents were divorcing and I felt like I was caught in the middle of a custody battle. I think I'd be hurting, but I wouldn't let anyone see that." The deeper the levels of mistrust, the longer it will take. Keep in mind that you are not addressing the resistance so you can get to work. The resistance is the work.

Genuineness

One challenge with working with clients that are resisting is that you will likely feel annoyed, irritated, frustrated or inept. Those feelings drive us to do things to protect ourselves, too. We get snarky, dread these sessions, and blame the client. The danger in this is that it reinforces what the client fears, and therapy becomes unsafe.

Reframing how we understand clients and resistance helps. Instead of resistance, we see hurting people trying to protect themselves the best way they know how, which heightens our empathy. Instead of feeling like we are terrible therapists, we recognize that working through the resistance may be the most important work we do with these clients, which helps us genuinely see the resistance as the work. As we see the resistance as an attempt to meet core needs, we develop more unconditional positive regard for our clients.

Therefore, part of working with a client's need to resist the work is a self-awareness about how it triggers our own needs. Perhaps a therapist likes to help others because it gives her inner value and makes her feel worthwhile. That works fine until she feels like she cannot break through a client's resistance to help, and then she doubts her worth. Then, she begins doing things to reaffirm *her* worth … and it is now about the therapist's needs, not the client's needs. The problem is not that the therapist has an unmet core need to be valued and worthy. We all have our stuff. The problem is when the therapist's needs supersede the client's needs and result in behaviors that negatively impact the client.

Since we all have core needs, this is a gentle reminder that therapists need to do their own work, too. These needs do not generally surface when our clients think we are awesome. They surface when the therapy is seemingly thwarted, when we do not feel like we are making progress.

When Is Creative Play Therapy Not a Good Treatment Choice?

Although we love Creative Play Therapy and have seen impressive outcomes with this treatment, it is not the best treatment choice for all clients at all times. While therapy may be beneficial for the individual, it may have unintended consequences in the family system. It can go very deep, and it can leave a client raw and exposed if not used properly. It can quickly get to core needs that a client is not yet ready to address.

Creative Play Therapy is not a good treatment choice if the client does not want to do it. If it is too outside the box, too risky, or too invasive to the client, then trust that the client knows best and do something else for now. Without using creative approaches, explore the resistance and learn what the client needs to protect. Or, just trust that the client knows what is needed.

When clients are in the middle of a painful situation, they may be in what we like to call survival. For example, when a loved one is dying, the client is not ready to process the grief because the client needs everything they have to still go to work, care for children, savor the time left and prepare for the impending loss. Digging deep into the emotional response could require using emotional energy that is more needed elsewhere. All clients are different, but if you find a client cannot seem to go deeper, it may because their current life situation requires all emotional coping skills to survive for now. Creative Play Therapy may be more appealing and useful after the situation stabilizes.

Any time physical safety is at risk, those safety needs are more important than deep healing work. Sometimes, they will work together, but you may need to do more traditional talk therapy safety planning and suicide or homicide assessments before returning to the creative work.

Creative Application: Procrastination

Procrastination is resistance to doing something. Have you ever considered how resisting might be a way to protect yourself? You resist that commitment because you know that you do not really have time for it, despite all those good reasons to do it. All that mental anguish about having to do it might be your body telling you to step away from the commitment. You resist starting a project too soon because finishing it on a tight deadline makes you feel accomplished ... or you resist starting too early because if you are rushed, you cannot do your best work, and that protects you from believing you are not good enough, since you can blame it on running out of time.

Consider something that you have been procrastinating. What is the why behind your own behavior? How is your resistance an attempt to meet a core need? How can you address that need and thus reduce the procrastination? Did you know that procrastination is actually your body communicating with you, trying to keep you safe?

Creative Technique: The Wall

Walls are great metaphors because they protect what is inside from threats outside, but they also may imprison what is inside. Both things happen with resistance. It is an attempt to protect, but it may also impair the client, distancing them from things that would be helpful. This technique is about externalizing the resistance. To explore both sides of the wall, request the client to construct a real wall with cardboard blocks, a paper drawing, miniatures in a sand tray, or other expressive art. Ask the client to add what is being resisted or from what the client needs protection. Then discuss how it is both a protective wall and an imprisoning wall.

Clients, at times, resist helping work because the perceived costs are too great. They need safety and security, but they may also have other unmet core needs. While resistance may be challenging for the therapist, reframing it as part of the client's work, not something to get through before starting the work, helps maintain unconditional positive regard.

Exploring Spirituality **14**

We could not write this book without addressing spirituality. In full disclosure, we both teach at a faith-based university where faith and spirituality are part of the curriculum, but it is also central to who we are as practitioners and people. We also believe that it is important for full healing to occur. Understanding a client's belief system is part of assessing resources, and everyone has one whether they believe in a deity, sacred texts, an organized religion or not. As practitioners, our personal belief systems are also part of our self-care, so spirituality is important for both client and therapist.

Healing from deep pain may change belief systems, too, and those changes for clients may impact relationships with larger family and cultural systems. Contemplating spiritual questions may require great courage to wade into the murky waters. Voicing questions and turbulent emotions out loud may seem sacrilegious or eternally dangerous, yet this process is about illuminating what is internal and suppressed.

In this chapter, we will use general terminology so that our message is accessible and adaptable. We freely acknowledge that we have specific beliefs which undoubtedly influence how we understand this topic, but we also readily accept that you, the reader, and clients may have different beliefs. Our aim is to encourage you to comfortably explore spiritual concerns with your clients as needed, not to sway you to our way of believing. As an attempt to do that, we will use the following terms:

Deity – a spiritual being or construct that is either internal or external to the person. For us, this is God, Jesus and the Holy Spirit, but it includes Allah, Hindi, Mother Nature, Inner Wisdom, a Higher Power, the Self and others.

Sacred Texts – These are collections of writings that form the basis of a system of beliefs. For us, this is the *Bible*, but it also includes the *Torah*, *Book of Quran*, Confucianism, poetry, inspirational quotations and others.

Spiritual Beliefs – unique, personal understandings of deity and sacred texts which may or may not be similar to a person's identified religion or spiritual community. If a person does not believe in an external deity or sacred texts, that is part of the person's spiritual belief system.

Spirituality – a relationship with a higher being or form of consciousness existing outside of the five senses and open to individual interpretation. It may include a religious affiliation or a generalized belief system (Hughes, 2011).

Existential Questions

When you work with people in pain, part of the meaning making is exploring existential questions, and they are often tied to core needs. These are difficult questions with complex and personal answers. Why am I here? How can my deity allow bad things to happen? What do I believe in light of this event/ trauma?

If safety and security has been compromised through rape, murder of a loved one, or the diagnosis of a brain tumor, what does that mean about a deity? Could it have been prevented with omniscient power, and if so, why was it not? Or, if you believe in random events, what does it mean when these things happen to you personally? How do you trust the beliefs of the past when dangerous things happen? When innocent people die or are severely hurt, how can that be understood in light of this belief system? Is there anything looking out for you and your loved ones? What keeps you safe and can it be trusted going forward?

When power and control are lost in natural disasters, car accidents or addictions, how can they be regained? How do you recover from being powerless? What if you feel rage toward a deity that allowed this to happen, since anger is often part of grief? How can you express anger when you blame yourself? Who really has the power to determine your life? Do you have a voice that is heard by powers greater than yourself? Is it possible to communicate with a deity? Are there limits to the deity's ability to intervene? What if you believe in a higher plan, but your desires are in conflict with that plan? What if the plan requires pain, and how does that coexist with goodness and peace?

Many spiritual issues relate to inner value core needs, too. Does the deity exist? Is the deity aware of personal pain or only aware at a global level? Do you matter in this life or beyond it? Are you special and cherished? What gives you purpose? If you think you are now tarnished, damaged or unworthy, how does that change your relationship with your deity or higher power? Is value internal or external and how does that relate to your belief system? Who/ What do you rely on to heal? Where do goodness and kindness fit when you have experienced evil? What if good and bad are blurred?

Finally, relationship core needs also have a spiritual component. Family metaphors are often applied to deity characteristics. Gender and intimate partnership norms are part of belief systems and sacred texts. How do you reconcile beliefs of being created by a deity, but with characteristics that are in opposition to being accepted by that deity? What if you feel abandoned, unwanted or uncared for by a deity? Loneliness and isolation may also be experienced spiritually. How do you understand intimate involvement with the spiritual world? Does love change or diminish over time?

As you see, these are extremely difficult questions to answer, and clients will come to different answers depending on the spiritual belief system they had growing up, their current beliefs, and the conclusions they move toward as they wrestle their ways through the questions. Even facing these questions is not without risk. Clients may become firmer in their beliefs, but they may also conclude that they no longer believe what they once did. This change may impact relationships with parents, partners and children. It could change career choices, living situations and identity.

Yet, Creative Play Therapy is a process to explore all these issues. This treatment provides a place to externalize these big, existential questions, to test out changes in beliefs, to sit with them, feeling the emotional and physiological impact, and to integrate spirituality with thoughts and feelings. Therapy is a safe place to say things that may have been unspeakable before.

Exploring Worth and Value

"Tell me about some of your spiritual beliefs," is a good way to begin to explore spirituality with your client. Then, you can use terminology that the client uses, and it informs your follow up questions. Be careful about assuming that similar terminology to your own means similar beliefs, but also avoid being excessively worried about offending the client. Like other topics, if you have created a safe space and are genuinely trying to understand, then if you say something that is untrue for clients, they will correct you.

Worth and value are existential concepts that are usually deeply embedded in spiritual beliefs. How people see themselves may reflect their beliefs about how a deity sees them. If, for example, a client believes that a deity is punitive and watching for any missteps to discipline, worth and value are necessarily linked to acceptable actions. On the other hand, if a client believes that a deity is unconcerned with individuals, then the client may not believe that he matters in that distant relationship. Worth and value may be intrinsic or extrinsic, based on clients' spiritual beliefs, as well as what they believe they deserve.

If you are working with clients with inner value core needs, exploring spiritual beliefs is especially important. This is often where perceived value or lack of value originates. Because of this, it may seem unchangeable ("Who can change God?") or a double bind ("What if God created me gay, but hates me because I am?"). This is why it is important to investigate the beliefs, say (or show) them out loud, and explore the implications. It is also why it may be terrifying to do so.

Exploring Purpose

People describe purpose as something bigger than themselves. Whether they attribute it to the Universe, the Law of Attraction or God's Plan, it is a spiritual belief. Purpose is some rational reason for why something happens, and many people find identifying purpose to be helpful in meaning making.

A client who concludes that having acid thrown in her face has made her more compassionate toward others has ascribed a purpose to her pain. Those who channel their own misfortune into creating organizations to help others with similar experiences create a purpose for their misfortune. When people say that they would not want to repeat an experience, but that they would not change it if they could, they have healing for the hurt. Gratitude for the struggle is a hallmark of resilience, and it, too, gives the pain a purpose (Thomas, 2009).

Finding purpose is the not the method to healing, but it is the by-product of moving through the stages of Creative Play Therapy to healing. Listen for hints of it during meaning making. Trying to find purpose before feeling the pain results in trite platitudes. Finding purpose in deep pain is a spiritual experience.

Redeeming Personal Pain to Help Others

Helping professions attract people who have often had deeply painful experiences. Sometimes, those helpers are seeking their own healing. Sometimes, they want to give what they did not receive. Sometimes, they want to use their experience to help others. Still-wounded helpers can be dangerous to others, but those who have healed from their wounds are often the most competent at facilitating the journey for others.

My (Dr. Denis') philosophy of counseling derives directly from sacred text. It describes God as "the God of all comfort, who comforts us in all our troubles, so that we can comfort those in any trouble with the comfort we ourselves receive from God" (2 Corinthians 1:3–4, New International Version). It is how I have found purpose in my own pain. I encourage students to view personal pain, trauma and failures as a strength that aids in helping others. My mini-speech that I give to every new cohort goes something like this:

> We all have stuff, our hurtful experiences, pain and things that scar us, but this stuff can be your strength. If you work through your stuff – and working through it is key – then on the other side, you are better equipped to help others because you get it on a level that others are not capable of. Your stuff makes you more compassionate, empathic and understanding, so celebrate your stuff and the difficult work to get through it. Hard stuff isn't shameful; it is what makes you a better helper.

Therefore, I want to charge you, the helper, to do your own work without the expectation that it will make you perfect. Imperfections are part of being relatable, so they, too, are valuable in healing work. Deeply feel your own emotions, learn to understand your emotional and somatic expressions, and make meaning from your own pain. Do the work that you ask your clients to do, but do your work on your own time so that you can be fully present with your clients.

Once you have reframed your own healing journey through pain to something positive that increases your ability to help others, you can now boost that resource for others.

Client:	So, I was talking to a friend the other day, and she confided that she had also been part of a cult.
Therapist:	What was that like for you to hear that?
Client:	It was weird. I knew exactly what it was like, all the ups and downs. I understood what drew her in, and why it was hard to leave. It brought back a lot for me, but I also could see how far I have come.
Therapist:	You got it because you've been there.
Client:	Yeah. I mean, it wasn't the same one, so some things were different, but so much of what happened was similar. I tried to encourage her because, see, I did it.

Therapist:	If you can do it, she can, too.
Client:	Yes! It felt really good to be able to help someone else. It almost makes it worth it to have been through all that crap.
Therapist:	One thing that changes all the bad stuff into something positive is being able to help another person.
Client:	I didn't think it was possible to change it into something positive, but I can see that starting to happen. Do you think I can do something good with all this?
Therapist:	The more important question is … do you?
Client:	I have been thinking about starting an organization to help survivors.
Therapist:	You know from experience what people need.
Client:	I do, don't I?

We often will do things for others that we will not do for ourselves, and this characteristic may be what makes finding purpose in pain by using it to help others so rewarding. It is the spiritual experience of comforting others with the comfort we ourselves have received.

Ethics

Because our belief systems are integral to who we are and because we may find comfort in them, they have, even with good intentions, been harmfully inflicted on clients. As an example, Section A.4 of the American Counseling Association's Code of Ethics (ACA, 2014) explicitly warns about avoiding harm and imposing values, stating, "Counselors are aware of – and avoid imposing – their own values, attitudes, beliefs, and behaviors" (p. 5).

Clients must explore their own belief systems and be free to come to their own conclusions. Like other areas, our role is to understand it from their perspective, not ours. We have found that this gives us more liberty to explore spiritual issues in session, since we respond with the same empathy and unconditional positive regard that we would for any other topic.

Creative Application: I Believe

To explore and know your own spiritual belief system, create a digital journal of photos and captions that capture what you believe. Find photos on the internet or take ones on your device that show what you believe to be true. Then, write that belief in a short caption. For example, I might find a photo of a wounded soldier carrying an injured comrade to safety. I would add the caption, "My stuff makes me compassionate and better able to help others. God redeems pain, bringing beauty from ashes."

This creative application is based on your belief system, so it does not matter whether others agree or disagree. You do not need to show it to anyone else unless you choose to do so. You may discover that things you want to believe in, or believe in theory, do not feel authentic when you try to add them to your journal. You may also find that things you once believed are no longer true for you. Externalizing and clarifying internal beliefs will likely be challenging, but illuminating.

Creative Technique: Nature Mandala

Nature is one way to introduce spirituality into sessions, since how we view and interact with nature often reflects our belief system. Mandalas, from the Sanskrit word for disk, are circular or other geometric shapes and are considered spiritual practice, reflecting infinity and wholeness through the circle. However, you do not need to introduce these lofty concepts with clients. Simply go outside to a confidential natural space and ask the client to create a circular piece of art with objects from nature. If it is not appropriate to go outside your office, gather pinecones, sticks, rocks, feathers and other natural objects for clients to use in your office. You can also use a creative prompt from Chapter 7 for a nature mandala.

All people have spiritual belief systems, and they can be helpful resources and part of the healing process. Spirituality can help with finding purpose in pain. However, wading into the murky waters of existential questions, anger toward a deity, or questioning cultural beliefs can be risky. It is important that therapists are aware of their own belief systems and remain open to exploring a client's unique belief system.

References

ACA. (2014). *2014 ACA code of ethics*. Alexandria, VA: American Counseling Association.

Hughes, B. (2011). The creative use of spirituality to enhance psychotherapy. *VISTAS*. Retrieved from http://counselingoutfitters.com/vistas/vistas11/Article_101.pdf.

Thomas, D. (2009). *Reaching resilience: A multiple case study of the experience of resilience and protective factors in adult children of divorce*. (Ph.D. Dissertation), University of Tennessee. Retrieved from https://trace.tennessee.edu/utk_graddiss/649

Creative Play Therapy and Self-Care   **15**

We could begin this chapter with dire warnings about the dangers of not taking time for self-care. We could cite the literature on vicarious trauma, burnout and compassion fatigue. We could caution about the threat of a shortened career in this field after all your years and expense of schooling and gaining experience. However, in our experience, students and practitioners do not need to be convinced of the importance of self-care. They need to be convinced to actually do it.

While preparing to leave town on sabbatical to write this book, I (Dr. Denis') spent countless hours sprucing up our house to prepare it as a short-term rental. We bought a new refrigerator to replace the leaky one we put up with for six years because it still worked. We bought new, beautiful bedding and furniture. We hired someone to deep clean it until it sparkled and others to fix our list of repairs. We did all this for strangers that we would never even meet, knowing that we would not have done it for ourselves.

Challenges of Self-Care

That is how helpers often approach self-care. Like my list of repairs, we usually know what needs to be done, but unless it becomes urgent, it gets put off until later. We limp along catching small warnings like my leaking refrigerator, but since we can still handle our work load and since the perceived cost of time to address the problem seems high, we make do. We continue to meet others' expectations (or what we think their expectations are), while not doing the things that would make life better for ourselves and our families.

One of the things I am most looking forward to enjoying when I get home is an Airbnb-worthy home. Our home is beautiful now, and the person managing it while we are gone has added wonderful hospitable touches to ensure that guests have a comfortable, relaxing stay. I like comfortable and relaxing, too, so why did we not do this sooner? We put it off because of cost, effort and priority.

Cost

Making the repairs on our home cost thousands of dollars, and most of the time, it is challenging to spend large chunks of money. With self-care, one of the biggest costs is time. With so many things competing for time, it may feel like you are giving up the last scraps of free time to squeeze in a healthy activity which just seems like another task on the list. Instead, we opt for things that numb or avoid emotion. Then, we keep going without addressing what needs to be repaired.

Effort

Helping work is hard work. We take in horrific stories and pour ourselves into difficult journeys with clients through the darkest places of human nature. Greenwald (1967) wrote about his experience using play with adults:

> I was using play not only for my patients' direct benefit but also to make it possible for me to deal with their problems without undue suffering. It is not helpful to the sufferer to permit his difficulties to engulf the therapist. One of the reasons many patients cannot be helped is that they arouse such intense emotions in the therapist that he cannot cope with them.
>
> (p. 47)

This kind of work is full-time, but it often bleeds into our personal time, too, because we care about our clients. We falsely equate worry with caring. We think about them frequently, but unlike other professions, we cannot talk about our work with friends and family. We hold secrets, shared by our clients, without confidential outlets to process our reactions. Then, we have our own stuff, too. Finding appropriate ways to externalize our responses to client stories, while dealing with our own issues, may feel like it requires an insurmountable amount of effort when we are tired at the end of the day or the end of the work week. Coupled with the cost of time (and maybe money), many use ineffective coping strategies that help in the short term, but do not nourish and replenish for the future. Although promoting self-care is part of most counselor training programs these days, few practitioners have flexible, well-developed and adaptive plans for self-care that they can consistently implement (Thomas & Morris, 2017).

Priority

If you have committed the time and resources toward becoming a helper, then you know how to prioritize. You chose to invest in a degree instead of backpacking Europe. You chose to study instead of socializing with friends. You chose to finish a stressful slew of assignments instead of reading your favorite author's new book. That does not mean that you will not backpack in Europe, socialize with friends, or spend a relaxing evening reading, but it does mean that during that time, you chose one good activity over another good activity. After a day of seeing back to back clients, you have many choices, and you likely need a lot of them. You need to eat, drink, sleep, relax, do some personal development, pursue your hobby, interact with people you love, have alone time, talk to your friends, know what is happening in pop culture or the political scene, shop for groceries, and more. Since it is impossible to do them all at the same time, you have to prioritize. The challenge is prioritizing self-care when it feels indulgent and selfish.

What Is Self-Care?

Before we talk about how to overcome the obstacles to self-care, first we need to determine what it is. Many of us have an image of bubble baths and candles after an 18-mile run, and while those things

The Definition of Self-Care

Self-care is nourishing and rejuvenating. It improves overall energy, clarity and health. It nurtures the whole person, physically, mentally, socially and spiritually. It is not avoidance or numbing to feel better in the present, but compassionate care of the self in the present to maintain or improve health in the future.

might be self-care, they also might be just the opposite. If you are hiding in the bathtub to avoid a conflict with your partner, spent $150 dollars on candles when your car is about to be repossessed, or chastise yourself with every step you run, then what could be soothing and energizing is not. Therefore, we define self-care not by the activity, but by the result.

A self-care activity reduces stress and increases health in one or more of four domains: physical, mental, social or spiritual. In my observation, the most successful self-care activities, the ones that become habits, are activities that combine multiple domains, are flexible, and include a friend (or pet). You are probably painfully aware of the areas that need the most self-care, but do not overlook the things you are already doing that are nourishing and rejuvenating. Self-care should feel good, not always be focused on weaknesses.

Neff (2015) has written extensively about the concept of self-compassion, and it is integral in self-care. One of the most nourishing and healthy things you can do that will have a domino effect in all domains of self-care is to develop compassionate self-talk. When internal dialogue is critical and harsh, it dampens the benefits of healthy activities. Do you talk to yourself with unconditional positive regard? You are valuable with inherent worth, just as your clients are! You deserve kindness and gentleness, especially from yourself.

If you are interested in learning how to develop a comprehensive self-care plan, you can read *How to Create a Wellness Plan That Works* to walk you through 100 days to create a personalized plan (Thomas, 2019). Below is a short summary of the seven parts (see also Figure 15.1).

Maintenance & Prevention: This is the foundation of a healthy wellness plan and the first area to address. These are the basics needed consistently (probably daily) to maintain wellness in all domains.

Figure 15.1   Seven Parts of a Wellness Plan

Restoration: You can often predict when stress will increase. That means you can also plan recovery from those stressful times as part of your wellness plan.

Emergency Strategies: While you cannot always plan when you may have an emotionally heavy client or an upsetting email, you can plan that unanticipated stressors will happen. Having a stash of quick, easy to implement strategies helps.

Challenges: Knowing yourself and understanding your own unique personal, perceptual and professional challenges helps you fortify those areas.

Record Successes: Keeping a record of how the work you do makes a difference provides a resource to review and remind you of your positive impact on others. Memory is not sufficient.

Support: By intentionally creating a small, supportive community of others who can mentor, challenge and encourage you, you add collegial, professional support for your wellness.

Self-compassion: The most nourishing wellness plans are surrounded by self-compassion. Guilt, shame and remorse over not doing the healthy things you "should" be doing undermines your health. Self-compassion counters the criticism from yourself and others and allows your plan to be more restorative.

How to Overcome the Obstacles to Self-Care

Before self-care can become a consistent replenishing of your health and energy, you have to decide what works as self-care and then do it. It is not easy, but we make it harder when we make the obstacles bigger and more difficult in our minds. How can you make it easier? Reduce the perceived cost and effort, and increase the priority.

Reducing the Cost

What do you see as the cost of doing the thing you most need for your self-care? Sometimes it is money, but cost also includes the resources of time, energy and stamina as well. It could include the cost of whatever you replace with a self-care activity.

Maybe you need to improve your physical health, but you think that working out an hour a day, six days a week, seems impossible, especially since it has been six months since you last exercised. You are probably right. Perhaps you could take a 10-minute daily walk instead. That would have added up to about 28 hours of exercise over that last six months, and most of us can find 10 minutes. Reduce the cost of time to something that is easy. Usually, 15 minutes or less is much less formidable when starting is difficult. Some is better than none. It is easier to add a little more time once you start, but the goal is not a buff body with new gym friends. The self-care goal is to feel nourished and rejuvenated in the present and/or the future.

Reducing the Effort

Capitalize on times when your energy is higher. What you do first thing in the morning always gets done, whether it is scrolling through your social media feed or meditating. That is helpful to know when building self-care habits. However, physical, mental and social energy wax and wane throughout the day, but in predictable patterns. Maybe you wake up slowly with your lowest physical energy of the day, but your mental energy is high when you are freshly awake. If you find journaling nourishing, do that first thing, but save physical exercise for later in the day. If, instead, your brain is tired after work or class, but your physical body is buzzing, plan movement when it will be most nourishing and rejuvenating, and do not expect that you will be willing to work on homework or case notes then. It costs less energy to do mental activities when your mental energy is high, physical activities when physical energy is high, and social activities when social energy is high.

Increasing the Priority

Why do you want to care for yourself? Which of your reasons motivates you? Perhaps knowing that self-care is something you *need* to do to feel better leaves you self-reprimanded, but not motivated to change. Many of us in this profession equate self-care with selfishness, and if candles and bubbles baths were just for you, well, it might be. However, our ability to care for ourselves directly impacts our clients, intimate partners, families and friends. You are the most important helping tool you have, and self-care is how you repair and sharpen that tool. When you do not, you become dull and broken from the work. Then, your work is less effective and your personal life suffers.

If you use Creative Play Therapy, you must build self-care into every week because this work is quick and intense. It brings out deep and painful wounds. When we contain and collect client pain, it is like holding a trash can out for them to dump their wounded stories. We provide the container for clients to express and eventually leave their hurt. Our job is to provide the safe space to contain their pain. However, as we hold that container, we will inevitably get splattered with some of the seeping wounds and feel the burden when it overflows. We see and hear the worst kinds of stories from our clients, and it inevitably impacts us, too. To extend the metaphor, we need to have consistent things in place to take out the trash. We need continual self-care.

We encourage you to build wellness into your schedule, just as you schedule time to complete case notes and block out client sessions. It is essential for career longevity, job enjoyment, client care and work/life satisfaction. You need self-care when you feel the urge to check out for a few hours, but by then you are already depleted. Instead, make deposits nearly every day to keep from running on empty, deposits that nourish and replenish. If you want to be a great helper, facilitate changed lives, and be an example of the healthy life you want for your clients, then wellness is not optional. Without it, you will limit yourself.

When addressing what later became the American Counseling Association, Carl Rogers (Rogers, 1980) concluded his speech with these words:

> ...The optimal helping relationship is the kind of relationship created by a person who is psychologically mature. Or to put it in another way, the degree to which I can create relationships which facilitate the growth of others as separate persons is a measure of the growth I have achieved in myself. In some respects this is a disturbing thought, but it is also a promising or challenging one. It would indicate that if I am interested in creating helping relationships I have a fascinating lifetime job ahead of me, stretching and developing my potentialities in the direction of growth.
>
> (p. 56)

By creating your own wellness plan (making it as flexible as needed), and consistently doing the things that increase your energy, nourish you inside and out, and relieve stress, you improve your growth potential. That makes you a better helper. Regardless of how depleted you are today, by consistently adding small deposits to your wellness bank, you will improve and develop reserves when you need them.

Do Your Own Work

It cannot be emphasized enough to do your own therapeutic work. We all have our stuff, so it is not shameful or weak to seek a professional to help. It may be liberating. It certainly helps us empathize better with the client's journey. Even poor experiences remind us why we want to be better helpers.

In addition to doing your work on your personal struggles, you need an outlet to process your response to client stories. When you hear vivid stories of perpetrators and oppressors, and you care for your clients, you will have a justifiable response. Though it may not be appropriate to share that response with the client, you need to be genuine about your own emotions. For example, after an intense session with a client, Dr. Denis' was putting away the miniatures that the client used in the sand tray. I squeezed the one used to represent the serial abuser and thought, 'I hate you!' I was surprised by my own strong reaction, and I knew I needed to get it out before I went home, so I did my own sand tray. (See the creative application below.) The client did not feel anger toward that person, but I did. By ignoring my strong response, it would likely seep in and contaminate my client's work, so I needed to metaphorically take out the trash. Others use music, intentionally selecting certain songs and genres on their commute to and from work to empty the trash can. Some have carved out a small painting studio and time each week to create and process this challenging work. You will need an outlet to do this, too.

Finally, be intentional with your transitions into and out of client work. Some practitioners find it helpful to have a routine that prepares them to sit with clients and then prepares them to leave client work in the office. For example, physically clearing your desk as a metaphor for clearing emotional space before greeting the client could be a ritual. Starting relaxing music, getting a drink of water, and eating a banana might work. If client work is broken up by, say, a staff meeting, then maybe taking a short walk around the building before going to your meeting aids with that transition. At the end of the day, you could review your client load for the day, write the emotions that you experienced on a piece a paper, and then slowly tear the paper into bits and leave it behind in the trash can. Some helpers use stoplights to remind them to take deep, relaxing breaths on the way home, and some stop at a convenience store to physically get out of their vehicle and transition out of work. When you do this, you better contain client work to work hours and work settings, limiting the draining bleed into your personal life.

Creative Application: Personal Sand Tray

One of the practitioners in our community who has worked extensively with childhood trauma shared her habit of creating a personal sand tray to process her responses. I have adopted that ritual at the end of the day to process clients and life concerns (they all happen together for the helper) before shutting the door to the office and heading home. Even though I do not process the sand trays with others, I found myself progressing through the stages to healing just from creating the sand tray, making changes, and putting it away. CAUTION: You may need to do this with a professional if it becomes too intense.

You can create a personal sand tray many different ways, but here is a suggested protocol to get you started.

1. First, begin with a smooth sand tray. If you have options, select the color of the sand and the shape of the tray that seem right to you today.
2. Without thinking about why, choose any miniatures or other objects that catch your attention and put them all in a basket or container.
3. Once the miniatures are gathered, arrange them in the sand tray in whatever way seems right, again avoiding thinking about why or what it might mean. (You want to stay in the creative right brain as much as possible for this portion.) You may or may not use all the miniatures you selected, and you may get ones that you did not originally select as you discover that you need to use them. This is your sand tray, and you know what you need.
4. When the sand tray is arranged the way it needs to be, pause and really look at it. Move to your analytic left brain and consider the relationships of the objects, what the sand tray is telling you, and how you physically feel. Sit with any emotions that arise. Label them and allow yourself to feel them.
5. Ask yourself, "What would I like to be different?" Then rearrange the sand tray to make any changes that you wish and are able to make.
6. Notice how it feels after the changes.
7. When you are ready, slowly put the miniatures away. Smooth the sand. Cover the tray and put it away, if you do that at your setting.

Creative Technique: Predicting Stress, Providing Wellness

Clients need to develop strategies for wellness, too. It strengthens the resources they have to do this therapeutic work. One empowering strategy is to predict high stress periods and plan extra wellness around those times. Instead of reacting to situations, clients learn to become proactive. (This works for helpers, too.) When clients anticipate a stressful event, such as going to court, mid-terms, or holidays with difficult family members, they know the date in advance. You can help them brainstorm what things would reduce the stress before arriving, during the event, and after it is over. Then, regardless of how it turns out, your client has maintained autonomy and some control.

You can explore options through a creation or through more traditional problem solving. The point is that anticipating does not mean worry, and the client is not powerless, even when others are making decisions outside of the client's control. This reframes the situation, changing the perception even if the situation does not change.

Taking Care of Self to Care for Others

Name: Angelyn
Age: 64

While I spend my working hours carefully providing a safe and non-judgmental environment for clients to engage in expressive activities, I often feel my working environment does not feel safe or nonjudgmental. As the pressures for client numbers increase, I find myself waiting for someone to give me permission or time off or retreats to engage in self-care ... which is, actually, "other" care. This focus results in no "other care," thus no self-care.

My left brain is saturated with facts, numbers and critical input. My right brain needs some release. My endorphins and serotonins need replenishing! To self-care, I need to hold space for myself in order to continue my own awakening and growth.

I do this by remembering to engage in an activity that helps me to regain my balance. Maybe it is painting, walking in the mountains, taking deep breaths, or focusing on the horizon line and letting myself imagine for a minute, a time when the right brain is given the right-away!

A time when all else fades away.
A time that opens me up and reminds me.
A time that brings me back to myself again.

A student, Eric, once observed that play therapists seemed to be overall much healthier. We have yet to see research comparing the wellness of play therapists with other helping practitioners on this anecdotal observation, but we have noticed a similar pattern, along with greater longevity in the profession. Play therapists seem to have a healthier balance between work and personal lives.

Perhaps it is because in seeing this work so well with clients, those doing play therapy work naturally use playful and creative techniques with themselves. They recognize that it is not just fun, it is fueling the capacity to try new things, do deeper work, and help the next client. They worry less about professional image, and playfully engage with toys and expressive arts, boosting their professional effectiveness.

Playing and being creative is healing for the client, and beneficial for the helper.

Summary and Conclusion

Now you have learned about Creative Play Therapy. Because we all learn from those before us, in Part One, we described this treatment modality's roots in Carl Rogers' theory, child-centered play therapy and expressive arts. We presented materials and essential listening and responding skills. We detailed four core needs and how behavior is often a way to meet those needs. Finally, we introduced an overview of development.

Then in Part Two, we presented a seven-stage model of the therapeutic process to simplify an understanding of what to expect. Although clients will cycle through the working portion many times, all clients begin with the Warm Up and finish with the Ending. In between, you will prompt Creation, allow them space for Emotional and Somatic Expression, facilitate Meaning Making and experience Healing.

In the final section of the book, Part Three, we encouraged you to reframe resistance as an attempt by clients to protect themselves and to see it as part of their work. We discussed the importance of including spirituality in client work, especially regarding difficult existential questions. Lastly, we concluded with what needs to come first for helpers using Creative Play Therapy: self-care.

Throughout the book, we included practical techniques to use with clients, first person case studies and ways to apply the information personally. We strove to make this book easy to read and understand because the content you see and hear from clients is often complex and difficult. We genuinely hope that Creative Play Therapy makes your job easier and more rewarding, and that your clients experience healing.

Thank you, Dear Reader, for reading to the very end. We know that your time is valuable and you have many options in how to use it. It is humbling and honoring that you chose to spend your time learning from us. We find being educators to be a joy in a profession that changes lives for generations of lives. May your work be that impactful.

References

Greenwald, H. (1967). Play therapy for children over twenty-one. *Psychotherapy: Theory, Research & Practice, 4*(1), 44–46. Retrieved from https://search.ebscohost.com/login. aspx?direct=true&AuthType=sso&db=psyh&AN=1967-09008-001&site=ehost-live&custid=s8863735.

Neff, K. (2015). *Self-compassion: The proven power of being kind to yourself.* New York: William Morrow Paperback.

Rogers, C. (1980). *A way of being.* New York: Houghton Mifflin Company.

Thomas, D. A. (2019). *How to create a wellness plan that works.* Seattle: Amazon Digital Services.

Thomas, D. A., & Morris, M. H. (2017). Creative counselor self-care. *VISTAS Online, 2017,* 1–11. Retrieved from https://www.counseling.org/knowledge-center/vistas/by-year2/vistas-2017/docs/default-source/vistas/creative-counselor-self-care

Index

Entries in **bold** indicate tables, entries in *italic* indicate figures.

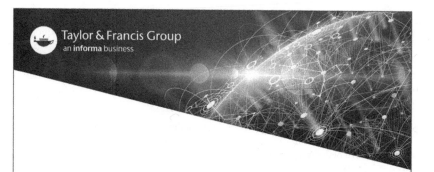